The Foundation Of Our Faith

Preparation For Membership
In The Moravian Church

KEVIN C. FRACK

The Foundation of Our Faith
Preparation For Membership in The Moravian Church

Copyright © 2007 by the Reverend Kevin C. Frack and
The Interprovincial Board of Communication
Moravian Church in North America
PO Box 1245, 1021 Center Street
Bethlehem, PA 18016-1245
800.732.0591
www.moravian.org

Book design: Anthony Gasparich
MC2, Lititz, PA

ISBN: 1-878422-65-0

Printed in the United States of America

CONTENTS

PREFACE

WELCOME TO A STUDY OF THE CHURCH. This material was written to answer basic questions about what it means to be a Christian and to prepare people for membership in the Moravian Church. For participants who come from other denominational backgrounds the study will provide a point of comparison. For those who have never belonged to a Christian Church, or who have not participated for a long time, the study will help you gain a personal understanding of the Gospel of Jesus Christ.

The information and exercises are intended to help you:
- Establish a common-ground understanding of basic Christianity
- Answer questions of faith
- Provide an environment to "experience" the Church through relationships developed during the sessions
- Initiate the practice of faith through spiritual disciplines and participation in congregational activities
- Help seekers determine their readiness for membership in the Body of Christ

The source of information about what God has to say to the Church and our world is the Bible. We call the Bible God's Word because we believe within these sacred writings, or Scriptures, the Lord has uniquely revealed Himself to people. The Bible is the standard of what we teach and what we believe, and therefore, the principle tool God uses to shape our lives. It will be important to have a Bible as you study. A variety of versions or translations of the Bible have been used in this study for exposure and comparison. Each translation of Scripture has its own strengths and weaknesses. Our goal is for you to experience that God is speaking to you. Your pastor or teacher will be able to advise you as to which translation of scripture will be most helpful.

This book does not pretend to be the definitive work on "Moravians." In fact, it leaves quite a degree of latitude for adding your own chapters to the story of God's work through your life. One of our assumptions is that God loves you and has created you with a purpose and inestimable value. Therefore, many of the sessions will have time for you to share as well as receive information.

More important than the materials in this study, it is the students whom God loves most. Therefore, while this study has been designed with eight chapters, adapting the tempo to the class is encouraged, depending on the needs of the participants. Those ready to explore membership seem to want more rather than less of the type of experience this study provides. It is not uncommon for groups to ask to keep meeting even after the material has been completed.

May God bless you with a hunger for more of the Good News of Jesus Christ to be revealed in your heart and life.

Chapter One

THE CHURCH

IF WE WERE TO TAKE A POLL of people on the street asking them to define *"the Church,"* we'd get as many answers as people questioned. Opinions are influenced by each one's personal experience with some aspect of church. The descriptions are both negative and positive. For some, church brings to mind wonderful memories of belonging, friendship and love, life changing experiences, growth, joy, and meaningful activities. For others, those memories include fear, intimidation, guilt, manipulation, preoccupation with money, boredom, condemnation, and even fighting. Sadly, the Church has sent some confusing signals over the years.

As we begin our discussion of the Church, it will be important to ask *"who's talking?"* Each personal set of experiences or lack of experience colors our attitudes as we approach the Church.

The Moravian Seal

GROWTH ASSIGNMENT

Take a few moments to list some of your own images of the Church, being careful to note how they may affect you today. What are some of the reasons or expectations that bring you to the Church at this time in your life?

*You'll find **Growth Assignments** throughout the book, these are optional assignments that can help you in your spiritual development.*

The fact that you are beginning a study of the Church is an indication that God may be working in you. Some of us have enormous obstacles and baggage to overcome merely to give God a chance to teach us some Good News for a change. Others are eager to get started because they know the Lord is opening a new door to endless possibilities. The variety of backgrounds, experiences, even feelings we bring to the start of our study is simply an indication of how very different we all are. We may bring little in common other than our mutual need for the Lord. Therefore, our definitions of church may reveal more about ourselves than about God. But it's where we must begin - exactly where we are.

As we take time to get to know one another, and hear what each of us thinks about the Church, let's listen to what God has to say. The Church was started by Jesus Christ.

IT WAS JESUS who called His first disciples to follow Him.

> *As he walked by the Sea of Galilee, he saw two brothers, Simon, who is called Peter, and Andrew his brother, casting a net into the sea - for they were fishermen. And he said to them, "Follow me, and I will make you fish for people." Immediately they left their nets and followed him.*
> *Matthew 4:18-20 (NRSV)*

IT WAS JESUS who taught them the example of His own life as the model for living.

> *I give you a new commandment: love one another; as I have loved you, so you are to love one another. If there is this love among you, then all will know that you are my disciples.*
> *John 13:34-35 (NEB)*

IT WAS JESUS who gave His life for our redemption from sin and for the salvation of the whole world.

> *But God demonstrates his own love for us in this: While we were still sinners, Christ died for us.*
> *Romans 5:8 (NIV)*

As explained in the preface, different versions of the Bible are used for exposure and comparison. Consult your pastor about which version may be the best for your needs.

The following abbreviations indicate which version of the Bible is being used. Please use this as your key throughout the study.

New Revised Standard Version (NRSV)

New English Bible (NEB)

New American Standard (NAS)

New International Version (NIV)

Revised Standard Version (RSV)

King James Version (KJV)

New King James Version (NKJV)

IT WAS JESUS who sent the Holy Spirit to empower the Church in its mission.

> *Nevertheless I tell you the truth: It is to your advantage that I go away, for if I do not go away, the Counselor will not come to you; but if I go, I will send him to you.*
> *John 16:7 (RSV)*

> *On one occasion, while he was eating with them, he gave them this command: "Do not leave Jerusalem, but wait for the gift my Father promised, which you have heard me speak about. For John baptized with water, but in a few days you will be baptized with the Holy Spirit."*
> *Acts 1:4-5 (NIV)*

IT IS JESUS who is Head of the Church and holds it together.

> *But speaking the truth in love, we are to grow up in all aspects into Him, who is the head, even Christ, from whom the whole body, being fitted and held together by that which every joint supplies, according to the proper working of each individual part, causes the growth of the body for the building up of itself in love.*
> *Ephesians 4:15-16 (NAS)*

IT IS JESUS who calls you as well. As the hymn by Samuel John Stone says:

> *The church's one foundation*
> *is Jesus Christ, her Lord;*
> *she is his new creation*
> *by water and the word;*
> *from heaven he came and sought her*
> *to be his holy bride,*
> *with his own blood he bought her,*
> *and for her life he died.*
> *(Moravian Book of Worship, Hymn 511)*

IT IS JESUS, therefore, who gives meaning to the word *"church."*

The biblical word directly translated to mean church is

the Greek word: *ekklesia*. We refer to the Greek language when talking about the New Testament, because it served as the universal language of the Mediterranean region during the time of Jesus. Most of the oldest written forms of the New Testament were written in Greek. Ekklesia literally means "the called out ones." It originally referred to the assembly of free citizens who were called out of their homes to make decisions affecting the life of the community.

A Variety Of Biblical Images Of The Church

Open your Bible to Matthew 16:15-19. What causes Jesus to give Peter a new nickname? Where did Peter get his revelation? What does Jesus say is the foundation of the Church? Is the foundation the man Peter, or the rock of his confession?

Look at 1 Corinthians 12:4-31. An early Christian missionary named Paul writes this letter to the church in Corinth. They had the tendency to divide one another into factions. What example does Paul use to illustrate how different parts and gifts can work together? What are some key principles for the Church to function as an inter-dependent community of parts? What holds us together?

Now turn to Ephesians 2:19-22. This is a letter also written by Paul to the young Christian church in Ephesus. What other descriptions does he use to describe "the Church?" Upon what foundation is the Church built? What imagery does he add in chapter 4:11-16?

Please find 1 Peter 2:4-10. This is another letter, possibly written by the same Peter who received the revelation about Jesus in Matthew 16. What additional descriptions of the Church does Peter add to ekklesia? Upon what foundation does Peter see the Church is built? What is the purpose of the Church in verse 9?

The very last book of the Bible is a vision of what God is yet to do. At the culmination of God's plan to restore his lost creatures, what picture does the writer paint in Revelation 21:1-5? How is the Church like the bride of Christ?

The Ground Of Our Unity

When Moravians talk about the Church, we summarize our understanding of what is most important in the document called, "The Ground of the Unity." There, we describe the purpose of the Church.

> *The Lord Jesus Christ calls His Church into being so that it may serve Him on earth until He comes. The Unitas Fratrum (an ancient name for the Moravian Church) is, therefore, aware of its being called in faith to serve humanity by proclaiming the Gospel of Jesus Christ. It recognizes this call to be the source of its being and the inspiration of its service. As is the source, so is the aim and the end of its being based upon the will of its Lord.*
> *(The Ground of the Unity, paragraph 1)*

The Heart Of What The Church Believes

From the very beginning, God has desired a relationship with people. In the first chapter of the Bible, after everything else had been made:

> *Then God said, "Let us make humankind in our image, according to our likeness; and let them have dominion over the fish of the sea, and over the birds of the air, and over the cattle, and over all the wild animals of the earth, and over every creeping thing that creeps upon the earth." So God created humankind in his image, in the image of God he created them; male and female he created them.*
>
> *Genesis 1:26-27 (NRSV)*

At the heart of the Church is an abiding awareness that we were made to enjoy God and glorify Him forever. When such an intimate relationship is absent, we experience the void of unfulfilled living. People coming to the Church often share that "something is missing" in life. The comment makes sense, especially if we're not doing what our lives were made for. The opening chapters of the Bible paint a picture of paradise, where people had nothing to hide and reflected God's image in everything. Apparently God is not the one with the problem. In the things that were made, God was pleased:

> *And God saw all that he had made, and it was very good.*
> *Genesis 1:31a (NIV)*

But in creating us, God loves us so much that we are not forced to reciprocate. Each of us has been given the capacity to accept, or reject, God's created intention for our lives. It is difficult for us to grasp love with no strings attached, because our love lives have so many painful reminders of unfulfilled expectations and manipulation. But the love God expresses by creating us with the liberty to make decisions is part of God's completely free, unmerited favor. In the Church, such love is called *"grace."* This is an amazing gift. To grant human beings an option to accept God's offer of grace, the Lord had to allow for the possibility that we would choose otherwise. And we did. . .

There are cracks in the picture of the whole and intimate connection God intends for us to know. Inherent within each of us is a desire to do things "my way." Each time human actions and decisions widen the gap between God's picture for our lives and our own, we experience sin. Sin is the Bible's way of talking about anything that separates us from God and what God intends. Every human being has been affected by the cumulative consequences of people making decisions contrary to God. The Psalmist puts it this way:

*God has looked down from heaven on the sons of men,
To see if there is anyone who understands, Who seeks
after God. Everyone of them has turned aside; together
they have become corrupt; There is no one who does
good, not even one.*

Psalm 53:2-3 (NAS)

The problem is that sin is killing us. Apart from God's picture for our lives, we only have a blurred and fading distortion. The end result of life apart from God is death. The writer of James describes the process of distortion of God's will through sin:

*But each one is tempted when, by his own evil desire, he
is dragged away and enticed. Then, after desire has
conceived, it gives birth to sin; and sin, when it is full-
grown, gives birth to death.*

James 1:14-15 (NIV)

GROWTH ASSIGNMENT

Perhaps you can think of a few very personal examples of how sin distorts the beauty of God's picture for your life. Why not take a few minutes and quietly ask God to change what sin has done in and through you? Who else has been affected by the separation from God you have experienced?

One of the most puzzling parts of being human with so many abilities is that we can actually recognize how far from God's way we have wandered, yet find ourselves unable to admit we need help. Out of wonderful intentions, people devise ways to *"get our acts together."* Whether through New Year's resolutions, self-help plans, quick-fix schemes, addictions, or perfectionism, people try to put all sorts of substitutes into that empty place God intends to fill in our lives, only to discover that nothing else satisfies. In fact, the truth is that we cannot save ourselves. No amount of human effort will suffice to bridge the chasm between where we are apart from God and where God wants us to be. Unless there is some change there is no hope for us.

Now for the Good News of the Gospel. It is one thing to learn that God really loves us. It is quite another thing to realize that God loves us even when we're lost in sin. God doesn't want anyone to be lost, or even to die apart from Him. And so, into the dilemma of sin that no human being can overcome, God sends the Promised One, wrapped in human flesh to reveal and restore God's plan of love. God sent Jesus to make plain in flesh and blood God's call for us to come home. Read Luke 15:11-32 to see how preoccupied God is with gathering His lost children:

> *And he arose, and came to his father. But when he was yet a great way off, his father saw him, and had compassion, and ran, and fell on his neck, and kissed him.*
> *Luke 15:20 (KJV)*

This story is not only about a child who was excessive in spending his inheritance, it's about our God and his lavish love being poured out for you and me. Imagine the Lord standing at the window watching and waiting for you to come home. At the first sign of your return **GOD RUNS** to welcome you in His arms! God rejoices at the interest you are showing in His plan to help us return to Him.

> *For God so loved the world that He gave His only begotten Son, that whoever believes in Him should not perish but have everlasting life.*
> *John 3:16 (NKJV)*

The life of Jesus teaches us how God wants to restore the original intimate relationship with us we were created to enjoy. It is not enough that Jesus was merely a great teacher. The teaching of Jesus and all the Old Testament only bring us to one conclusion: we are unable to overcome the power and effect of sin in our lives. Our involvement in sin has left us with a death sentence and debt of astronomical proportions. Look at Romans 6:23 and see what Paul has discovered about the penalty for sin. We are incapable of paying. But Jesus demonstrates the greatest act of love as He lays down His life in place of our own:

Greater love has no one than this, that one lay down his life for his friends.

John 15:13 (NAS)

The death of Jesus is God's own sacrifice once and for all, satisfaction in full for the penalty our own sin has incurred.

And by that will we have been sanctified through the offering of the body of Jesus Christ once for all.

Hebrews 10:10 (RSV)

It would be easy to become paralyzed with horror at what our sin has done to Jesus. But we would miss the purpose of God when he sent His Son. God's Good News is that at the death of Jesus Christ, full in the face of our need for a Savior, we are set free and can experience what Jesus has done to our sin! When Jesus died on the cross, He took every sin in the whole world - past, present, and yet to come - into His body. So when He died, Jesus effectively put to death sin's power over us. In every way, the down-payment of His life in place of ours buys us back from eternal death - it *redeems* us. His resurrection from the dead invites us to consider leaving behind our life lost in sin, set free to live as a restored participant in His kingdom forever.

God's Reason For The Church

God not only has a desire for individuals, but for community as well. The moment we come to His intended and most personal relationship we are no longer alone, but are made part of the community of all others who have been bought with the precious blood of Jesus. His goal is to make a people who are His own and who will reflect Him to the world. When new members are received into the Moravian Church, by Baptism, Confirmation, and Affirmation of Baptism, these words are proclaimed:

In grace God called and chose the people of Israel and established with them a covenant: I will be your God and you will be my people. In that relationship they were to

9

be freed from sin and become a blessing to all. Then God came to us in Jesus Christ and fulfilled that covenant for all people. Through Christ's life, death, and resurrection, God made for us a covenant of grace.
(Moravian Book of Worship, page 165, paragraph 1, and page 170 opening paragraph)

And so, we are back to the Church as the group of those who have responded to Jesus' call. The purpose of the life, death, and resurrection of Jesus was to call us personally to come back into full relationship with God and into full participation among the redeemed community.

But you are a chosen people, a royal priesthood, a holy nation, a people belonging to God, that you might declare the praises of him who called you out of darkness into his wonderful light. Once you were not a people, but now you are the people of God; once you had not received mercy, but now you have received mercy.
1 Peter 2:9-10 (NIV)

Getting Right With God

The grace God extends to us is limitless. In the Scriptures, God's grace - His unmerited love and favor - is spoken of as "boundless," "abundant" or "abounding," and a "free gift." Grace is frequently associated with faith - the response in us which accepts or receives the offer of God's grace. And even faith itself is the "gift of God's grace" to us.

For by grace are ye saved through faith; and that not of yourselves: it is the gift of God: Not of works, lest any man should boast.
Ephesians 2:8-9 (KJV)

It boggles the mind to realize that God's grace does not depend upon our performance. There is nothing we could do to cause God to love us more. In fact, there is nothing we can do to cause God to love us less. God's love and favor are part of His nature. "God is love." (1 John 4:16b)

Such un-earnable love is beyond our ability to comprehend. But, with God's help, it is possible to experience or "know" such love.

> *I pray that out of his glorious riches he may strengthen you with power through his Spirit in your inner being, so that Christ may dwell in your hearts through faith. And I pray that you, being rooted and established in love, may have power, together with all the saints, to grasp how wide and long and high and deep is the love of Christ, and to know this love that surpasses knowledge - that you may be filled to the measure of all the fullness of God.*
> *Ephesians 3:16-19 (NIV)*

As infinitely loving the gift of God's grace may be, we are not forced to respond to God's offer of salvation in Jesus. We can accept or refuse the offer of grace, even though the offer is never withdrawn. Moreover, Jesus promised to help us receive His invitation by sending the Holy Spirit (breath, essence) after He went away.

> *But the Helper, the Holy Spirit, whom the Father will send in My name, He will teach you all things, and bring to your remembrance all that I said to you.*
> *John 14:26 (NAS)*

The Easter Sunrise Service of the Moravian Church expresses the phenomenal work of the Holy Spirit with these words:

> *We believe that by our own reason and strength we cannot believe in Jesus Christ our Lord, or come to him; but that the Holy Spirit calls us through the gospel, enlightens us with gifts of grace, dedicates us to God, and preserves us in the true faith, just as the Spirit calls, gathers, enlightens, and dedicates to God the whole church on earth, which he keeps with Jesus Christ in the only true faith. In this Christian church God daily and completely forgives us and every believer all our sin.*
> *(Moravian Book of Worship, page 85)*

Therefore, when considering how we come to God, a better approach might be: "How does God come to us?" Our relationship with God always depends first on God's grace, "God's goodwill for our salvation" as Ancient Moravians put it. Even our ability to respond to God is a gift of God. The Holy Spirit works in our hearts and minds to draw us to Christ, as Lord and Savior, who is the ultimate way God comes to us.

There are as many varied responses to establish this saving relationship as there are individual persons. We speak of such things as sorrow for sin, repentance, faith, and consecration, but these are not a series of steps that everyone takes in a particular order in the same way. They are not merely a checklist that we can mark off and move on. These responses are all a daily part of our ongoing Christian life, our journey of faith with God.

If you sense that you need to respond to Christ's call, we believe the Holy Spirit is helping you to receive God's gift of salvation and to help establish you in a life with Him as your Lord and Savior. The Spirit helps, but God will not decide for you. Here are some responses the Scriptures teach us that may be helpful:

> **Repent** expresses several ideas: It is a change of mind, the experience of regret or remorse, and the turning away from sin back to God. It is the transformation from a life directed away from God to one turned around which seeks God. *Repent* is the first word of Jesus' sermon, when He says: *"Repent, for the kingdom of heaven is near."* (*Matthew 4:17*) The call to *repentance* is not a message of *condemnation*, but one of God's heart-broken pleas for His wayward children to come home. *Repentance* means to be so deeply sorry for disobeying God that we respond by *turning away* from our sin, and *toward* God in faith. *Repentance* is not only the event of turning to God for the first time, but a daily experience of returning to Him whenever we wander away.

Take a moment to talk with the Lord about any needs you have for repentance.

One of the gifts the Holy Spirit gives to restore our relationship with God is to *convict* us of sin. *Conviction* is neither a preoccupation of striving for personal perfection nor is it *condemnation*. Rather, *conviction* is the inner awareness of specific aspects of our lives which run contrary to God's will. These obstacles to our growing closer to the Lord are sin and must be removed for health and growth to continue. The Holy Spirit helps us recognize the problem of sin in our lives to lead us to *confession* and *forgiveness*. *Confession* is our response of agreement with God that sin is blocking our relationship with the Lord. In *confession* we name our sins and ask God's help and *forgiveness* to move past them as obstacles to our faith. *Forgiveness* is God's promise to treat us as though we have never sinned.

> *"If we confess our sins, he who is faithful and just will forgive us our sins and cleanse us from all unrighteousness."*
>
> *1 John 1:9 (NRSV)*

Take a moment to pray the words of Psalm 139:23-24:

> Search me, O God, and know my heart;
> Try me, and know my anxieties;
> And see if there is any wicked way in me,
> and lead me in the way everlasting.
> Psalm 139:23-24 (NKJV)

Spend some time in silence, seeking the help of the Holy Spirit to become aware of anything about your life which runs contrary to God's will. You may want to write them down.

Ask God to forgive you specifically for any sin you know is hindering the health and growth of your relationship with God, others, and yourself.

Re-write the promise from God's Word in 1 John 1:9, inserting your name and specific details where underlined. Then read it aloud for you to hear and receive the promise God makes to you.

"If <u>we</u> confess <u>our sins</u>,
he who is faithful and just will forgive <u>us our sins</u>
and cleanse <u>us</u> from <u>all unrighteousness</u>."
1 John 1:9 (NRSV)

Believe in Jesus Christ our Savior. North Americans think differently than biblical people. When asked what we believe, most people respond with what they think in their minds. Biblical culture, however, approaches belief more by what we do. To believe something, or have faith, is to commit one's life into action as though what we say we believe is true. For example, we may think a chair is behind us, but it doesn't become faith until we actually sit upon it. So it is with faith.

"And what is faith? Faith gives substance to our hopes, and makes us certain of realities we do not see."
Hebrews 11:1 (NEB)

Faith is accepting Jesus Christ's invitation to know Him as our personal Savior. Faith is trusting that His life, sufferings, death, and resurrection have actually brought us into right relationship with God. Faith is repenting and receiving the forgiveness and peace God promises. Faith is trusting Christ that we can begin a new life in Him. Faith is committing our lives to Him in the expectation that He will guide us, provide the gifts we need to serve Him, and be with us always, regardless of circumstance, forever.

"For I am convinced that neither death nor life, neither angels nor demons, neither the present nor the future, nor any powers, neither height nor depth, nor anything else in all creation, will be able to separate us from the love of God that is in Christ Jesus our Lord."
Romans 8:38-39 (NIV)

Repentance and faith together, in response to the gift of grace from God, produce a change in the sinner's condition and relationship with God. This we call *conversion*. Christ Jesus gives us a new heart, mind, will, and motive to live in gratitude and obedience to Him. This inner or spiritual experience is called *regeneration* or the *new birth*.

> "So if anyone is in Christ, there is a new creation: everything old has passed away; see, everything has become new." 2 Corinthians 5:17 (NRSV)

GROWTH ASSIGNMENT

Take some time to write your own personal prayer of faith for God to help grow your relationship with the Lord. What are some specifics about the person God created you to be - the "new creature" - that are different from the "old you." Are there any things about your life you believe God is inviting you to do or view differently?

Profession of faith is the open declaration of the faith in our hearts. The point of entry into the redeemed community of the Church is that place and time where you can publically confess or agree with God that you indeed have received God's grace and begun a new life in Christ. Saying aloud what God has done *"professes"* it for all to hear. We do this through the recognized rites of the Church, as well as by private testimony. Just as a couple being married has made careful preparations and personal commitments to one another long before their wedding ceremony, so the *public profession of faith* is the formalization of what has already occurred in the believer's heart and personal life. Acknowledging faith in Jesus as Lord and Savior is the public step which begins church membership.

> "And I tell you, everyone who acknowledges me before others, the Son of Man will also acknowledge before the angels of God."
>
> Luke 12:8 (NRSV)

In order to help formalize your statement of faith, the Moravian Church asks new members to publicly profess faith in response to the following question:

Do you believe in God as your Creator and loving heavenly Father, in Jesus Christ as your Savior and Lord, and in the Holy Spirit as your Comforter and Sustainer, according to the Holy Scripture?
I do.
(Moravian Book of Worship, page 170)

GROWTH ASSIGNMENT

Write in your own words your statement of faith. What have you seen and heard from God that is most important for others to know?

Consecration is the complete devotion of a Christian to the Lord God, impelled by grateful love. We give our lives and talents in service, obedience, and full submission to Christ. Being a member of the Church of Jesus Christ is not like joining a club. We are still fully human, and continue to need the grace of God to deal with sin yet undiscovered. But in responding to the Lord's invitation, we enter a lifelong process of being *disciples - those who follow and learn as they grow.* Joining the Church is a serious commitment, being "given over" to live the rest of our days in such a way as to learn to be more like our Savior in heart, soul, mind, and body. Such a dedication of our lives brings us not only into a local congregation, but also into the ranks of faithful saints through the ages.

Here is the question the Moravian Church asks publicly about your determination to live for Christ:

Do you in this faith turn away from sin, evil, and selfishness in your thoughts, words, and actions; and do you intend to participate actively in Christ's church, serving God all the days of your life?
I do.
(Moravian Book of Worship, page 171)

Re-write the previous question of commitment from the Moravian Book of Worship, turning it into your personal promise in response to God. Make it as specific, yet honest, as you can. What is the single most important step of commitment you believe God is inviting you to take today? Are there any areas where you know you will need help? Where can you find such help?

Methods Of Joining The Church

When we join the Church we are formalizing a process God has been working in us for a long time. It is our way of letting others know we have accepted God's gift of love and forgiveness in Jesus, and we promise to commit our lives in service and growth in His will. We are also asking for God's blessing and the support of sisters and brothers in the Church to help us as we follow and learn from Christ. This public declaration that we receive and reciprocate God's love and dedicate ourselves to his service is called *the profession of faith.* As in marriage, this public statement is a most significant promise. Therefore *it is not to be entered into unadvisedly or lightly but discreetly, thoughtfully, and with reverence for God.(Moravian Book of Worship, page 175)* There are several ways the church recognizes those ready for membership.

Adult Baptism

Baptism was practiced by Jewish people before the time of Jesus. Certain Jewish groups used ritual washing as a way of indicating to God their desire to be washed from any uncleanness which resulted from living in this world. One group, for example, the Essenes, washed many times daily to cleanse away the stain of sin. John the Baptist helped people practice such ritual washing. But John himself taught about the **Messiah** *(God's appointed deliverer)* saying:

> *I indeed baptize you with water; but one mightier than I cometh, the latchet of whose shoes I am not worthy to*

unloose; He shall baptize you with the Holy Ghost and with fire.

Luke 3:16 (KJV)

With Jesus, baptism becomes the outward act which indicates a person has repented and returned to God, while God has worked a permanent change on heart, soul, mind, and body. It is called a *sacrament* in the Moravian Church - *something we do on the outside that shows God is at work on the inside.* The Church baptizes new members because Jesus told us to:

"Go therefore and make disciples of all the nations, baptizing them in the name of the Father and the Son and the Holy Spirit . . ."

Matthew 28:19 (NAS)

We ask those joining the Moravian Church who have never been baptized and are ready to profess their faith to be baptized. The most important concern to us in baptism is obedience to Jesus' command to "baptize."(Matthew 28:19) Since the amount of water used is not specified in the Scriptures, the form of baptism is considered "non-essential." Therefore, all Moravians acknowledge that sprinkling, pouring, and immersion are equally valid. The person to be baptized is asked to kneel as a *watchword (a verse of scripture)* is read to guide or encourage his/her new Christian life. Water is then typically applied three times for the three ways we know God as Father, Son, and Holy Spirit. The sacrament is sealed as hands are laid upon the person, symbolizing the pouring out of the Holy Spirit.

The Moravian Book of Worship describes what God does on the inside as we profess faith and use water on the outside:

Our Lord Jesus Christ instituted baptism as the visible means of entry into the new covenant. Baptism is a gift of God. In this sacrament, through grace and the power of the Holy Spirit, we are united with Christ, are cleansed by his saving work, enter into the fellowship of the Church, and are called to a life of faith and willing obedience.

(The whole congregation is asked) Those of you baptized into Christ Jesus, how were you baptized?
Into his death. We were buried with him through baptism into death, so that as Christ was raised from the dead through the glorious power of God Almighty, we too might be raised to live a new life.
(Moravian Book of Worship, page 165)

The baptism of John was repeated whenever a repentant person knew the need for cleansing from sin. The baptism of Jesus is done only once. When baptisms were performed at the Jordan River, as the person went into the water, it was as though the old person living life apart from God had died and was being buried. As the person came up out of the water it was as though a whole new person was being born. In Paul's letter to the church in Rome, he says:

"Or don't you know that all of us who were baptized into Christ Jesus were baptized into his death? We were therefore buried with him through baptism into death in order that, just as Christ was raised from the dead through the glory of the Father, we too may live a new life."
Romans 6:3-4 (NIV)

For this reason, many converts to Christianity over the centuries actually received new Christian names to mark their transformed identity in Christ. Baptism into the death of Jesus is done only once, because we believe that Jesus' death paid a sufficient price to cover all the sins of the whole world forever.

He has no need, like those high priests, to offer sacrifices daily, first for his own sins and then for those of the people; he did this once for all when he offered up himself.
Hebrews 7:27 (RSV)

Therefore, whenever baptized Christians have a need to wash away sin they do not take another *water bath*, but revisit the broken body and blood of Jesus where He is still putting to death sin's power over us. The benefits of His redeeming work are still as powerfully at work today, whenever we realize and confess our sin and receive forgiveness. If you have been baptized in some other Christian church, we will not re-baptize you, since we believe that God acted in your baptism, regardless of how little you were able to understand about what God was doing.

GROWTH ASSIGNMENT

Take a moment to look at the paragraph describing what God does in baptism. What specific personal issue is God attending to in your heart and life with regard to each of God's works?

Baptism Of Children

The Bible does not speak directly to whether or not the Church should baptize infants. Scripture does, however, give some allusions to early Christians bringing their whole households for baptism (Acts 16:15, 33). As parents came to know Jesus as Lord and Savior, they began to bring their children to receive the benefits of being baptized into the death of Jesus. Since it is God who acts in the baptism based on faith that is only ever partially "understood" some believing families had their children baptized to signify that God was indeed at work in their lives. By the fourth century, the baptism of infants became widely practiced.

Moravian reformers of the mid-fifteenth century separated from Roman Catholicism to return to a more biblical practice of church life. The Church began a process over the years of examining its attitudes about baptism in light of the Scriptures. Moravians have come to affirm that:

> In baptism children also share in the benefits of our Lord's redeeming work through God's grace and the faith of parents, and of the Church, for God's promise is to us and to our children.
>
> (Moravian Book of Worship, page 165)

However, since scripture is not definitive on the matter of infant baptism, there remains the opportunity in the Moravian Church for some dialogue about baptism. The Moravian Church practices infant baptism for the same reasons we practice adult baptism - because Jesus commanded us to baptize. Therefore, it is the common practice of the Moravian Church that parents are encouraged to present their children for baptism. The "sacrament" is what we do as an outer sign that the true and inner work is being done by God. Baptism is a gift of God. We do not believe that baptism saves the child any more than we believe that baptism saves an adult. In fact, salvation rests upon God's grace offered to us in Jesus which is accepted and lived out by faith.

> *For it is by grace you have been saved, through faith - and this not from yourselves, it is the gift of God - not by works, so that no one can boast.*
>
> *Ephesians 2:8-9 (NIV)*

We believe that God loves children and cares for them eternally until they are able to make discerning decisions for themselves.

> *But Jesus said: "Let the little children come to Me, and do not forbid them, for of such is the kingdom of heaven."*
>
> *Matthew 19:14 (NKJV)*

We encourage parents prayerfully to invite the lordship of Jesus not only over their personal lives, but over their homes as well. It is an awesome responsibility for parents to profess their faith in Jesus for their families and then to commit to live in such a way as to help their children experience the love of God for them. Parents can invite other professing Christians, we call *sponsors,* to *"stand with them"* in such spiritual responsibility. In baptism, God enters into a covenant with parents, who enter a covenant with sponsors and congregation to join in providing a shield of Christian nurture and protection around each child, leading someday to their own *confirmation* of Jesus as Lord and Savior in their personal lives.

Parents and sponsors are asked:

Relying on the power of the Holy Spirit, do you promise to lead your children by prayer, instruction, and example toward that time when they can by grace confirm their faith in the Lord Jesus Christ and commit themselves to the life and work of the church?
I do.

(*Moravian Book of Worship, page 166*)

The whole congregation is then asked:

Do you receive and affirm these children of God as members of this congregation and accept your obligation to love and nurture them in Christ?
We do.

(*Moravian Book of Worship, page 166*)

Confirmation

When those who were baptized as children come to a personal and saving relationship with Jesus, they are asked to *confirm* or *affirm* their baptism. This gives the opportunity to make personal and public declaration of love and devotion to the Savior. It is a time where believers take personal responsibility for their life of faith as they are recognized as full partners in the ministry of the Church.

Young people typically have some time of teaching preliminary to confirmation to prepare them for fruitful membership in the Body of Christ. Confirmation, or *catechism* (teaching), instruction serves the same purpose as the material in this study. Older persons who have not publicly professed their faith, but were baptized as infants are also asked to *confirm* their relationship with the Lord.

The outward activity or *rite* performed in a confirmation service is very similar to an adult baptism, with the exception that no water is used. The same questions are used for profession of faith as were used in adult baptism. Confirmation ends with the charge from the pastor:

By affirming your baptismal covenant in public worship today, you have taken another step in your journey with God. You have entered into a new relationship with God and this congregation. We charge you in God's name always to remain faithful to Christ and the church, and to be open to the leading of the Holy Spirit.
                    (Moravian Book of Worship, page 173)

Reaffirmation Of Faith

Many people attending our study have been baptized and confirmed members of other churches, but for one reason or another, have been away from the Church for some time. As those who have fallen away from active participation in the life of the Church find their relationship with the Lord restored while in the Moravian Church, they are also asked to profess their faith in Jesus, using the same questions as those in adult baptism. It is an opportunity to start fresh.

Reaffirmation of Faith is a formal way to tell the Lord and the Church that one of God's wandering children has come home. Individuals are not re-baptized nor confirmed, but restored to a previous place of grace and belonging. The pastor welcomes you home with the charge:

You have affirmed your faith and baptismal covenant before God and this congregation, and, by the grace and strength of Christ, have declared your desire and promise to renew your Christian discipleship. We welcome you with joy and thanksgiving. May the Lord be with you. Build yourselves up on your most holy faith, led by the Holy Spirit. Keep yourselves by grace in the love of God, as you wait for our Lord Jesus Christ in his mercy to give you eternal life.
                    (Moravian Book of Worship, page 173)

Transfer Of Membership

Some participating in this study have been active members of other Christian churches. It is the understanding in the

Moravian Church that your previous church membership has been simply in another part of God's kingdom, which we recognize as part of the larger Body of Christ. We ask that those wishing to transfer their membership contact the pastor of their previous congregation to forward a *Letter of Transfer*. During the service which receives new members, we invite those transferring their membership to participate, also, in the profession of faith. This gives an opportunity to let the local congregation know of their relationship with Jesus and commitment to serve Him among the community of faith here.

The pastor publicly welcomes those transferring membership with the following:

Through baptism, profession of faith, and Christian service, you have already entered into the life of the Church Universal, and today we rejoice to welcome and receive you into the fellowship of this congregation. Continue faithfully in the good way you have chosen in Christ, and may the Holy Spirit bless you in your life among us. May we all, through grace, be enabled to support and encourage one another in Jesus Christ our Lord.

(Moravian Book of Worship, page 173)

Chapter Two

THE STORY OF GOD'S PEOPLE

WHEN MORAVIANS ARE ASKED TO RESPOND to the question "What is a Moravian?" the answer will likely come in the form of a history lesson. In fact, the Church has learned that God reveals His love for us in very real and historical ways. The story of God's love for people is much older and broader than the Moravian Church, yet recent and specific enough to include you. It begins and ends with God as the only source of our life and salvation. We get our information about how God initiates and cultivates His relationship with people from the Bible. Moravians describe how we view God and His Word as follows:

> *The Triune God as revealed in the Holy Scripture of the Old and New Testaments is the only source of our life and salvation; and this Scripture is the sole standard of the doctrine and faith, of the Unitas Fratrum and therefore shapes our life.*
>
> *(The Ground of the Unity, page 4)*

The Bible is important to us because amidst the limited words of human language we sense the very presence of the infinite God showing Himself to us. The Bible is not an ordinary book. We must approach the scriptures (sacred writings) with great care, because they were not written with the same purpose as books today. The Bible is the quintessential love story. Our Creator is constant in His invitation for human creatures to know Him and grow through imperfect glimpses of His eternal love. The Old and New Testaments are God's promises or covenants with us, written so we would always remember God. The record of God's revealing work to people in the past fills the present and future with hope and anticipated joy.

> *Hear, O Israel: the LORD our God, the LORD is one. Love the LORD your God with all your heart and with all your soul and with all your strength. These commandments that I give you today are to be upon your hearts. Impress them on your children. Talk about them when you sit at home and when you walk along the road, when you lie down and when you get up. Tie them as symbols on your hands and bind them on your foreheads. Write them on the doorframes of your houses and on your gates . . . be careful that you do not forget the LORD, who brought you out of Egypt, out of the land of slavery.*
>
> *Deuteronomy 6:4-12 (NIV)*

The first accounts of scripture were not written. In fact, until the time of Moses, the memories of peoples' life changing experiences with God were passed on by word of mouth in the form of a memorized *oral tradition*. After Moses led the Hebrews out of slavery as the newly redeemed *people of God* the oral accounts began to be put into written form in the Hebrew language. As Greek culture came to dominate in the Mediterranean region, Hebrew scriptures were also translated into Greek. Scribes took great care in copying scrolls to preserve as accurately as humanly possible the remembrance of God's activity with people.

The earliest New Testament accounts were also *word of mouth*. Those who knew Jesus personally simply told what they had seen Him do and heard Him say. As those first disciples aged and the Church spread, eyewitness accounts were written down to preserve the teachings and to speed the dissemination of Jesus' story. Actually, the oldest New Testament books are some of Paul's letters of advice to young Christian churches. The New Testament was primarily written in Greek, since it was the predominant language of international communication during the first century of the early church.

With time, sixty-six books were recognized by the Church as being uniquely inspired by God. Even though its contents reveal the human experience of God over more than 2000 years on three different continents, the Bible is really only one story. This story of God's self-revealing work in the scriptures is the *canon*, or *measuring stick* of our present practice of faith. It is the story of God's love for people, of people's response (or lack thereof) to God, and then God's sacrificial and ongoing plan to save us from the consequences of our disregard for God. Let's get familiar with your Bible with an overview of God's message.

> *All Scripture is inspired by God and is useful for teaching, for reproof, for correction, and for training in righteousness, so that everyone who belongs to God may be proficient, equipped for every good work.*
> *2 Timothy 3:16-17 (NRSV)*

The Journey Begins

The first five books of the Bible are known in Jewish tradition as *The Law* or *Torah*. They teach us how we got here, what God did to bring us together, and how He expects us to live as a godly community. Imagine sitting among the nomadic Hebrew campsites, around the fire after a long day walking the Sinai Desert asking the question: *"How did we get here?"*

Genesis (the beginning) tells us that God made everything, including people, with His seal of approval:

> *God saw everything that he had made, and indeed, it was very good.*
> *Genesis 1:31a (NRSV)*

God works in a very tangible world. The blessings and goodness of His creation were not theoretical, but meant to be experienced and celebrated in very spiritual, physical, emotional, and intellectual ways. God's attitude toward us, as seen in Creation's intention, is *very good*. It is in Creation that God displays His plan for intimate relationship with His creatures. It is into Creation that He steps, in the flesh *(incarnation)* to make the way back to God, taking God's Word of promise and making it a knowable, historical reality:

> *And the Word became flesh and dwelt among us, full of grace and truth; we have beheld his glory, glory as of the only Son from the Father . . . No one has ever seen God; the only Son, who is in the bosom of the Father, he has made him known.*
> *John 1:14-18 (RSV)*

If God's Creation displays His plan and salvation to us, it also becomes the battle ground in which we learn our need for God. Paradise only lasts for two chapters in Genesis before we find out why life is not a *Garden of Eden* for us. Sin *(separation from God)* enters the scene in Genesis, chapter 3, by way of Evil's temptation and human disobedience, and follows in nearly every chapter thereafter. When God's intended blessing is replaced with the curse of sin's consequence, Creation itself suffers with us:

> *Cursed is the ground because of you; In toil you shall eat of it All the days of your life. Both thorns and thistles it shall grow for you; And you shall eat the plants of the field; By the sweat of your face You shall eat bread, Till you return to the ground, Because from it you were taken; For you are dust, And to dust you shall return.*
> *Genesis 3:17b-19 (NAS)*

The rest of the Bible is the saga of the human struggle with sin and its consequences and the Lord's intervention to bring people back into closeness with God. In the next chapters of Genesis, not only have God's creatures lost their intimate relationship with their Maker and His blessings, but we see the deterioration of human relationships, as well. Adam and Eve were tempted to *"become like God."* They teach us that sin causes human hearts to take matters into their own hands, living to serve themselves and the gods their own hands would make. Genesis emphasizes how utterly distasteful sin is to God. The way people live their lives is an indication of what position God plays in human hearts. Since we were made to honor God first, any other *"first-love"* offends the Lord.

> *The LORD saw that the wickedness of humankind was great in the earth, and that every inclination of the thoughts of their hearts was only evil continually. And the LORD was sorry that he had made humankind on the earth, and it grieved him to his heart.*
>
> Genesis 6:5-6 (NRSV)

As God planned to cleanse sin from the world we find an amazing discovery. In the midst of a world of sin, some few righteous still live to serve God!

> *But Noah found favor in the eyes of the LORD. This is the account of Noah. Noah was a righteous man, blameless among the people of his time, and he walked with God.*
>
> Genesis 6:8-9 (NIV)

God's affection for a remnant of faithful ones becomes the foundation of His covenant promise: "to you who are faithful and love me, I will *"save or preserve"* you from destruction of your sin and restore you to a blessed relationship with Myself." In every time of history, God raises up those who love Him enough to show others the way back to God. While human inclination would be to eradicate tainted Creation, God promises to *"redeem and restore"* that which has been distorted by sin. God loved His world so much, when the time was right, He Himself would enter His own Creation to take on our flesh and blood to remove the curse of sin forever.

*God loved the world so much that he gave his only Son,
that everyone who has faith in him may not die but have
eternal life. It was not to judge the world that God sent
his Son into the world, but that through him the world
might be saved.*

John 3:16-17 (NEB)

The Journey Begins

About 4,000 years ago, God asked Abram and Sarai to trust
Him on a journey. Their response brought their whole
family into a unique relationship with God. They were so
transformed by following God's direction, the aged couple
received new names *(Abraham and Sarah - Genesis 17)*. God
chose this obscure tribe of nomads to bless the world. He
wanted Abraham and Sarah's descendants to be so
different as a people that the whole world would know
about God through them. They even had to learn to trust
God to give them a son when they were in their nineties.
After disastrously taking matters into their own hands to
have a son *(Ishmael)*, they laughed in disbelief when God
promised to give them descendants like the stars of the sky
through the son He would give them. To remember God's
goodness over their unbelief, they named this son *"Isaac -
he laughs."*

GROWTH ASSIGNMENT

See if you can find a map in the back of your Bible which shows the
journeys of Abraham from Ur of the Chaldeans to Haran to Canaan to
Egypt and back again to Canaan. Imagine what it might take for you to
leave your world behind to trust God and follow Him to a place He
would show you? Have you ever had to take such a journey of faith?
What happened? What did God teach you along the way?

Abraham and Sarah could not pass on the personal and
transformed nature of their relationship with the Lord to
their descendants. In fact, each successive generation
would have to learn for itself about the importance of
walking with God. Abraham and Sarah's grandson was
named Jacob. He was a deceptive fellow who tricked his

twin brother, Esau, out of the birthright to lead the clan. Even Jacob's name means *"the deceiver."* After many years of hiding in a foreign land, God called Jacob to return to the land of his father, Isaac. It was dangerous, because Esau had grown rich and powerful. The night before they were to meet, Jacob wrestled all night with the Angel of the Lord. Have you ever spent a sleepless night struggling over something you perceived God wanted you to do? Jacob was never the same. In the morning, the Lord gave Jacob a blessing, a dislocated hip and a reconciled relationship with Esau. His name was changed to *"Israel - he struggles with God."* From this time the children of Abraham, Isaac, and Jacob became known as *"Israelites - the people of Israel."*

Much of the Old Testament is the demonstration of the Lord's incredible patience with rebellious or complacent people. God's recurrent theme is the call for us to make decisions: *choose disobedience and suffer the consequences, or seek and return to God and witness Him turn even our worst human folly into a blessing.* Joseph, Abraham's great-grandson, became the second most powerful leader in Egypt. He got to Egypt, however, because his jealous brothers sold him to slave-traders just to be rid of him (Genesis 37-50). When famine struck the land of the Israelites, they wound up, hat-in-hand in Egypt, looking for food. When Joseph realized his own estranged brothers had come for food he reconciled with them and invited the whole clan of his father, Jacob, to move to Egypt. And thus, the stage was set for one of God's great interventions in human history.

> *And as for you, you meant evil against me, but God meant it for good in order to bring about this present result, to preserve many people alive.*
>
> *Genesis 50:20 (NAS)*

The Exodus And The Law

Exodus, the Going Out book, begins after a space of about 400 years. Circumstances have changed. The land which had once been a haven of food and safety for the Hebrews was enslaving God's people. What happens when people cry out to God?

> *During that long period, the king of Egypt died. The Israelites groaned in their slavery and cried out, and their cry for help because of their slavery went up to God. God heard their groaning and he remembered his covenant with Abraham, with Isaac and with Jacob. So God looked on the Israelites and was concerned about them.*
>
> Exodus 2:23-25 (NIV)

God not only heard their groaning and remembered His promises to their ancestors, *He perceived their suffering intimately.* A rather comical scene unfolds in Exodus chapters 3 and 4 when God called Moses to lead his enslaved people out of bondage in Egypt. Why choose Moses? He is tending sheep, hiding in the land of Midian because of his criminal record for murder. Moses is afraid, he is 80 years of age, has difficulty speaking in public, doesn't have a reputation as a leader with the people, and he doesn't even seem to know God until the Lord reveals Himself as *"I Am Who I Am"* (Exodus 3:14). But this is the story of God and what the Lord can do with anyone. Moses was never the same after he obeyed God's voice. Those who follow God are changed forever as we get to know the God who personally intervenes in human history to save and restore His children.

> *Now if you obey me fully and keep my covenant, then out of all nations you will be my treasured possession. Although the whole earth is mine, you will be for me a kingdom of priests and a holy nation.*
>
> Exodus 19:5-6a (NIV)

GROWTH ASSIGNMENT

Take a moment to reflect on some personal reasons you may have as to why God couldn't use you in service. Are there any excuses you make regularly when asked to participate in God's work? What might God say to you about what He can do even with your inadequacies? Can you make a list of some special gifts God may have given you to use for Him?

A Simple Pattern For Living

See if you can find a map in the back of your Bible that shows the Exodus. Can you find the Wilderness of Sinai? What would be some of the obstacles facing such a large number of people on the move through the desert? Have you ever found yourself in such a desperate position you had to trust God for even the simplest things?

The Exodus is among the most memorable events in human history. God formed a nation at Mt. Sinai with those who had followed into the wilderness. There, Moses received ten commandments as the framework to govern how God's people would live together. This *Law* became the symbol of what would make them different from all their neighbors. *Exodus, Leviticus, Numbers, and Deuteronomy* give considerable attention to defining the Ten Commandments in detail for daily living. Jesus called this the first and greatest commandment. (Matthew 22:37)

> *Hear, O Israel: The LORD our God, the LORD is one. Love the LORD your God with all your heart and with all your soul and with all your strength. These commandments that I give you today are to be upon your hearts. Impress them on your children. Talk about them when you sit at home and when you walk along the road, when you lie down and when you get up.*
> *Deuteronomy 6:4-7 (NIV)*

Can you list the ten commandments found in Exodus 20:1-17? Which of these seem most difficult? Why do you suppose God would give such a list to His people? How might these commandments help us in areas of living not listed here? How do the teachings of Jesus affect these ten commandments?

Moving Into The Promised Land

Part of God's promise to Abraham was to give the land of Canaan as a permanent home for his descendants. Unfortunately, as God's people got ready to claim their *Promised Land*, they became afraid and lost their trust that God would help them defeat their enemies. They rebelled against God and Moses. As a result, the Israelites were forced to wander the desert for forty years until all those who failed to believe, including Moses, had died (Numbers 13&14). The book of Joshua tells how the children of Israel, after the years of wandering, worked to occupy their *Promised Land*. It is difficult to justify any Good News from a loving God amidst accounts of warfare and bloodshed. But the theological message is clear: *those who remain completely devoted to God will be blessed, while those who compromise the relationship of faith in order to be like their neighbors can lose their experience of God's nearness!* Joshua's farewell address is a plea to younger Hebrews:

> *Now if you are unwilling to serve the LORD, choose this day whom you will serve, whether the gods your ancestors served in the region beyond the River or the gods of the Amorites in whose land you are living; but as for me and my household, we will serve the LORD.*
>
> *Joshua 24:15 (NRSV)*

GROWTH ASSIGNMENT

Can you find a map in the back of your Bible that shows the early years of Israel moving into the Promised Land? How many of the tribes can you identify? Can you find the city of Jericho? Who are some of their neighbors? Can you imagine why some of their neighbors became their enemies? What are some of the issues that arise when someone new moves into your life? How could you pray for the modern inhabitants of this same land who seem to have so much difficulty living side by side?

From Judges To Kings

For the next several hundred years, the Hebrew people were stuck in a cycle of disobedience and its consequences, followed by obedience, followed again by disobedience. As long as a strong person of faith led the people, there was prosperity and safety. However,

> *after that whole generation had been gathered to their fathers, another generation grew up, who knew neither the LORD nor what he had done for Israel. Then the Israelites did evil in the eyes of the LORD and served the Baals.*
>
> *Judges 2:10-11 (NIV)*

When the suffering caused by their sin became unbearable, the people cried out to the Lord, and God *raised up* a deliverer to restore them in faith. These leaders of faith and unusual charisma were called *Judges*, because they helped God's people know the difference between faithful and unfaithful living. The scriptures introduce us to some ordinary people of God who stepped forth in bleak times to become extraordinary leaders of faith *(Othniel, Ehud, Shamgar, Deborah, Gideon, Tola, Jair, Jephtha, Ibzan, Elon, Abdon, Samson)*.

The last of the judges was Samuel. Throughout *Judges*, the Israelites were a loosely connected collection of 12 tribes with a common faith. The people, however, wanted to have a king like their neighbors. Samuel was the reluctant prophet called by God to initiate a new way of living.

The books of **Ruth and 1 & 2 Samuel** describe what God desires in a leader. *Saul* was unusually big and strong and was anointed the first king of Israel. But unlike other nations, Israel's kings were always under God's authority. When Saul disobeyed God, Samuel was told to anoint David king.

> *But the LORD said to Samuel, "Do not look on his appearance or on the height of his stature, because I have*

rejected him; for the LORD sees not as man sees; man looks on the outward appearance, but the LORD looks on the heart."

1 Samuel 16:7 (RSV)

The Kingdom Of Israel

It is David's heart that catapults him to become the *apple of God's eye.* He was far from perfect - he had an affair with another man's wife, had the husband killed when she got pregnant, was father of a deeply tumultuous family ... Yet God saw in David the repentant spirit of a man *after God's own heart.* Many of the **Psalms** are attributed to David as he expressed his love and need for God.

What might this Psalm cause you to consider about your relationship with God?

*O LORD, our Lord, how excellent
is Thy name in all the earth!
Who hast set Thy glory above the heavens.
Out of the mouth of babes and sucklings hast Thou
ordained strength because of Thine enemies,
that Thou mightest still the enemy and the avenger.
When I consider Thy heavens, the work of Thy fingers,
the moon and the stars, which Thou hast ordained,
what is man that Thou art mindful of him,
and the son of man that Thou visitest him?
For Thou hast made him a little lower than the angels,
and hast crowned him with glory and honor.
Thou madest him to have dominion
over the works of Thy hands;
Thou hast put all things under his feet:
All sheep and oxen, yea, and the beasts of the field;
The fowl of the air, and the fish of the sea,
and whatsoever passeth through the paths of the seas.
O LORD, our Lord, how excellent is
Thy name in all the earth!*

Psalm 8 (KJV)

It was David who consolidated the territory of Israel under his rule and enforced peace with surrounding nations. It was David who moved the capital to Jerusalem to create a center of both government and worship. It was David whom God inspired to build a permanent temple, (even though his son, Solomon would actually build it). A thousand years before the birth of Jesus, it was to David that God promised a descendant would always sit upon the throne.

GROWTH ASSIGNMENT

If you were to write a Psalm, pouring out the deepest things on your heart to God, what would you include? Take a few moments to express yourself to the Lord.

It was not an easy succession of power for the children of King David. David wasn't even dead while several sons manipulated events and people to secure the throne. Solomon succeeded in obtaining David's blessing. The books of **Kings and Chronicles** relate the succession of kings who followed David. Solomon is largely remembered for his building programs and great wisdom. When asked by God what Solomon would like God to give him, Solomon replied:

> *"So give Thy servant an understanding heart to judge Thy people and to discern between good and evil. For who is able to judge this great people of Thine?"*
>
> 1 Kings 3:9 (NAS)

The books of **Proverbs, Song of Solomon, and Ecclesiastes** are credited to have grown out of Solomon's *wisdom literature.* Under his leadership, the nation extended its boundaries even further than under King David and became an international power, attested to by the countries of origin of his many wives.

What might you do differently in thinking about the future if the following wise sayings were true in your life:

*Trust in the LORD with all your heart, and
do not rely on your own insight.
In all your ways acknowledge him, and
he will make straight your paths.*
Proverbs 3:5-6 (NRSV)

*There is a time for everything,
and a season for every activity under heaven:
a time to be born and a time to die,
a time to plant and a time to uproot,
a time to kill and a time to heal,
a time to tear down and a time to build,
a time to weep and a time to laugh,
a time to mourn and a time to dance,
a time to scatter stones and a time to gather them,
a time to embrace and a time to refrain,
a time to search and a time to give up,
a time to keep and a time to throw away,
a time to tear and a time to mend,
a time to be silent and a time to speak,
a time to love and a time to hate,
a time for war and a time for peace.*
Ecclesiastes 3:1-8 (NIV)

The Divided Nation

As wise and powerful as he was, not even Solomon was above God's call to undivided devotion. The Bible remembers him as the king whose wives led him astray by *"turning his heart after other gods"* (1 Kings 11:4). The consequence of Solomon's compromised faith found the nation of Israel on the verge of civil war. After Solomon died, his son Rehoboam was unwilling to make amends for his father's practices. As a result, the ten northern tribes broke away to form the nation of Israel with its capital in Samaria. The Southern kingdom left to Solomon's descendants maintained control over Jerusalem and was called **Judah**.

Can you find the map in the back of your Bible that shows the two kingdoms of Israel and Judah? Can you find their capitals of Samaria and Jerusalem? Who are some of their powerful neighbors?

Alongside the historical account of God's people, the Bible also includes the messages of the **Prophets.** *Prophets* are people with an unusual insight into what is on God's heart and mind. We tend to associate prophets as those who predict the future. Actually, prophets hear God so clearly they are able to state the consequences of listening to God or of *hardening our hearts* in disobedience. Prophets are inspired by God to be a spiritual conscience to the official government, society, and religious practice. In the Bible they were also God's messengers of hope to a discouraged nation. Their purpose is always to call God's people back to God.

Some prophets did not write or have their utterances recorded. The writing prophets are grouped into two types: *major and minor.* The distinction refers to the volume of their writings, not to the value of the message. The books of the prophets are the last books of the Old Testament.

Elijah, Elisha, Obadiah, Jonah, Amos, and Hosea were active as agents of God in the century after the division of Solomon's Kingdom. They attempted to save the people from their own self-destructive behavior. However, the northern kingdom was judged guilty of disobedience when it was destroyed in 722 B.C. by the Assyrians.

The southern kingdom continued for about another 130 years. Prophets **Isaiah, Nahum, Micah, Zephaniah, and Habakkuk** saw God's judgment on an international scale. While the Assyrians were seen as God's judgment on the northern kingdom, Babylon was seen as judgment on Assyria. **Jeremiah and Ezekiel** preached desperately to avert similar disaster for Judah, to no avail. Jerusalem was destroyed by the Babylonians in 586 B.C., and the Jewish leaders were carried off as captives into exile in Babylon.

Sometimes prophets spoke specific words of judgment toward situations of their day. What might Hosea say today in light of his message?

> *Hear the word of the LORD, you Israelites, because the LORD has a charge to bring against you who live in the land. There is no faithfulness, no love, no acknowledgment of God in the land. There is only cursing, lying and murder, stealing and adultery; they break all bounds, and bloodshed follows bloodshed. Because of this the land mourns, and all who live in it waste away; the beasts of the field and the birds of the air and the fish of the sea are dying.*
>
> *Hosea 4:1-3 (NIV)*

At other times prophets told of a better future that the Messiah would bring. What encouragement might you gain from such a promise?

> *And it will come about after this that I will pour out My Spirit on all mankind; And your sons and daughters will prophesy, Your old men will dream dreams, Your young men will see visions. And even on the male and female servants I will pour out My Spirit in those days. And I will display wonders in the sky and on the earth, Blood, fire, and columns of smoke. The sun will be turned to darkness And the moon into blood, Before the great and dreadful day of the LORD comes. And it will come about that whoever calls on the name of the LORD will be delivered.*
>
> *Joel 2:28-32 (NAS)*

Captivity In Babylon

During the 50 years of captivity in Babylon, **Daniel** paints a picture of life far from home, and the challenges of remaining faithful to the Lord at all costs. With no temple to focus religious activity, the synagogue arose as a more local center of faith in a foreign land. The *captivity* became a time of great introspection and purification for the

Hebrews. Prophecies of restoration raised the hope that someday, when their punishment was complete, Jerusalem (Mt. Zion) would be rebuilt.

> *As a mother comforts her child, so I will comfort you; and you will be comforted over Jerusalem. When you see this, your heart will rejoice and you will flourish like grass; the hand of the LORD will be made known to his servants, but his fury will be shown to his foes. See, the LORD is coming with fire, and his chariots are like a whirlwind; he will bring down his anger with fury, and his rebuke with flames of fire.*
>
> Isaiah 66:13-15 (NIV)

GROWTH ASSIGNMENT

Can you find a map in the back of your Bible that depicts the kingdoms of Babylon and Persia? They represent the next major players to affect the history of God's people. Have you ever felt yourself caught up and swept away in events too large for you to control? Make a list of some specific situations where you or others have felt completely helpless. Ask God what you would most like the Lord to do? What do you think God's answer might be?

Rebuilding Jerusalem

A new day dawned when Persia conquered Babylon and the Jewish people were given permission to rebuild Jerusalem (538 B.C.). Rebuilding Jerusalem was slow. It took over 100 years. The descendants of those who were not carried off to Babylon still living near Jerusalem created great problems. Because they had intermarried with non-Hebrews, they were viewed by those returning from captivity as having compromised the true faith. As a result, fighting erupted that stalled the reconstruction. *Ezra and Nehemiah* are the historical accounts of the rebuilding efforts.

Life was so good under Persian rule that many Hebrews chose not to return to Jerusalem. The book of *Esther* relates what life was like for those Hebrews who continued to live far from Israel. Even in a period of relative peace, with permission to inhabit Jerusalem, there was a growing sense

41

of incompleteness in Judaism by the end of the Old Testament. Four hundred years before the birth of Jesus, hope was growing for God's *Appointed One,* **the Messiah,** to usher in a new age with the establishment of God's Kingdom. *Haggai, Zachariah, and Malachi* paint the picture of expectation, setting the stage for God's New Covenant.

> *"Behold, I send my messenger to prepare the way before me, and the Lord whom you seek will suddenly come to his temple; the messenger of the covenant in whom you delight, behold he is coming," says the LORD of hosts.*
> *Malachi 3:1 (RSV)*

GROWTH ASSIGNMENT

What is the longest you have ever had to wait for a promise to be fulfilled? What was it like during the waiting? What changed about your attitude once the promise was fulfilled? What are some promises you believe God would like to fulfill in and through your life? How is your attitude now about God's promises yet to be realized? What will you do while you wait?

Era Of Expectation - Between The Testaments

There are nearly 400 years between the end of the Old Testament and the beginning of the New. During this inter-testamental period great events were happening on the world stage. In 333 B.C. Alexander the Great defeated Persia and ushered Greece to the fore as the major international power. Even though his rule was brief, and his empire was divided into four pieces, *Hellenism,* or Greek culture, began to dominate the Mediterranean region. Initially, Jews were given special consideration and freedom to practice their faith. The Old Testament was translated into Greek (called the Septuagint) around 250 B.C. in order to help a growing international Jewish community to remember God. However, when Judaism was prohibited in Palestine in 175 B.C., great discontent erupted.

There are 15 books, called *The Apocrypha,* which detail life in Israel during this turmoil. Unlike the Old and New

Testaments, *the Apocrypha* is not considered by Protestants to be authoritative in the same way as the Old and New Testaments. However, this literature does help to give insight into the Jewish desire for an independent kingdom. Under the Maccabees, Palestine revolted in 167 B.C. and succeeded in establishing a free Jewish nation. The Jewish festival of *Chanukah* comes from the celebration of this victory and the rededication of the Temple.

However, by 63 B.C. a new power appeared on the scene: Rome. Roman armies invaded, took Jerusalem, and desecrated the Temple. They entrusted local government to local royalty who could curry the favor of Rome. Herod the Great, a non-Jew, was the ruler of Palestine under Roman authority at the birth of Jesus. A despicable character who had many of his own family members murdered, as well as the babies in Bethlehem (Matthew 2:16), Herod was also a great builder. In order to ingratiate himself with his Jewish subjects, his most memorable project was the rebuilding of the Temple in Jerusalem. In the midst of a terrible king's reign God saw the time was just right to send *the Messiah*, and with Him, bring near the Kingdom of God.

GROWTH ASSIGNMENT

Which characters of the Old Testament stand out most in your mind? What is it about their life with God that helps you? Is there any particular book of the Old Testament you find most interesting? How does God use that book to grow your faith? What is most confusing to you about the Old Testament? Why not spend some time asking God to help you know what He wants to show you in such places?

Chapter Three

GOD'S PROMISE BECOMES FLESH

THE STAGE WAS SET. Anticipation ran high on many fronts among different factions of the Jewish people that God would send a deliverer. Some, such as the Pharisees, expected that the deliverer would save them from sins. Others, like the Zealots, were waiting for a military leader to deliver them from the power of Rome. Some, like the Sadduccees and Herodians, would rather not rock the political and religious boat. Like most groups of people in most times, there was great diversity of hope as Jesus came into the world.

The New Testament opens with four accounts of the life of Jesus. These four books are called *The Gospels,* or *Good News.* Similar in content, in that each shares the account of knowing Jesus as the promised *Messiah,* each is also distinct and represents a unique perspective on the Savior of the world. The original followers of Jesus were not as concerned with detailing a written documentary of the life of Christ as they were preoccupied with being with Him and then telling the story of what they had seen and heard of Jesus. It was only after those who knew Jesus personally began to age and die that the Church recognized the need to collect together authentic accounts of Jesus' teaching.

Matthew, Mark, Luke, and John each bring the memory of *Emmanuel - God With Us.*

Mark appears to be the oldest written form of the Gospels, presenting a streamlined, *"just the facts,"* account of Jesus' ministry. *Matthew and Luke,* very similar to Mark, are the only two Gospels that begin the story of Jesus with his birth. Matthew speaks much about Jesus' fulfillment of Scripture's promise and our obedience to the commands of Christ. Luke brings a more cosmopolitan world view, reflecting deep understanding of Jewish faith, yet with an ease in Greek to explain faith to a non-Jewish world. *John* is the most different of the four. John takes the most explicitly theological approach to the life and teachings of Jesus. The longest sermons of any of the Gospels are in John. One of their purposes seems to be to deal with early forms of *gnostic* thought. *Gnosticism* (from the Greek word *to know*) was a popular intellectual approach which disdained the body and was driven by the aim to rise above the flesh to mentally capture an elevated understanding about God. *Gnostic* thinking threatened the simple and biblical teachings of Jesus that salvation comes through a relationship *with* God, who *redeems* our bodies, rather than secret knowledge *about* unseen things.

It is amazing to realize that Jesus never traveled very far. With the exception of his childhood journey to avoid the murder of babies in Bethlehem by King Herod, Jesus' travels were confined to Palestine. His main language was Aramaic. On the surface, the carpenter from Nazareth seems a most unlikely candidate to fulfill any promise, let alone to change the world for all eternity. Many very religious people missed recognizing Jesus, because he didn't fit their preconceptions of what the *Promised One* would look like.

GROWTH ASSIGNMENT

When you imagine Jesus, what picture comes to mind? How well do you know the Savior? Do you recognize any differences between the Jesus of Scripture and your own expectations? Turn to the Gospel of John 1:10-13.

He was in the world, and though the world was made through him, the world did not recognize him. He came to that which was his own, but his own did not receive him. Yet to all who received him, to those who believed in his name, he gave the right to become children of God - children born not of natural descent, nor of human decision or a husband's will, but born of God.

John 1:10-13 (NIV)

Do You Know The Savior?

When Paul wrote the letter to the church in Philippi, most of the four Gospels were not yet in written form. While encouraging the young church, he calls us all to have the attitude or *"mind"* of Christ Jesus. In what some scholars believe may have been an early church hymn, Paul recounts essential elements of who Jesus is and why Jesus came to this world.

Your attitude should be the same as that of Christ Jesus: Who, being in very nature God, did not consider equality with God something to be grasped . . .

Philippians 2:5-6 (NIV)

Jesus Is God

The Old Testament prophets laid a foundation of expectation that the demoralized state of God's people would change dramatically through the direct and personal intervention of the Lord. Throughout the writings of Isaiah a theme is repeated of God's promised coming:

Strengthen the feeble hands, steady the knees that give way; say to those with fearful hearts, "Be strong, do not fear; your God will come, he will come with vengeance; with divine retribution he will come to save you."

Isaiah 35:3-4 (NIV)

Behold, the LORD has proclaimed to the end of the earth, Say to the daughter of Zion, "Lo, your salvation comes; Behold His reward is with Him, and His recompense before Him."

Isaiah 62:11 (NAS)

At the core of each Gospel is the recognition that Jesus is the Promised One of God. John begins His Gospel with the clear affirmation of Who Jesus is.

In the beginning was the Word, and the Word was with God, and the Word was God. He was with God in the beginning. Through him all things were made; without him nothing was made that has been made. In him was life, and that life was the light of men. The light shines in the darkness, but the darkness has not understood it. . . The Word became flesh and made his dwelling among us. We have seen his glory, the glory of the One and Only, who came from the Father, full of grace and truth.

John 1:1-5, 14 (NIV)

While Mark records no birth narratives, the simple Gospel begins by picking up Isaiah's expectation. John the Baptist is seen as preparing the way for Jesus, the Lord.

Here begins the gospel of Jesus Christ the Son of God. In the prophet Isaiah it stands written: "Here is my herald whom I send on ahead of you, and he will prepare your way. A voice crying aloud in the wilderness, 'Prepare a way for the Lord; clear a straight path for Him.'"

Mark 1:1-3 (NEB)

When Jesus asked His disciples if they knew who He really was, Simon Peter replied,

"You are the Messiah, the Son of the living God." And Jesus answered him, "Blessed are you, Simon son of Jonah! For flesh and blood has not revealed this to you, but my Father in heaven."

Matthew 16:16-17 (NRSV)

We have the advantage of looking back at the first coming of Jesus through hindsight which includes all He did for us and the memory of 2,000 years of the Church. Those who met Him when He arrived had to *"see for themselves."* For many, Jesus didn't fit their expectations that when God came to earth, He would do so in a *"God All Mighty"* manner. Jesus claimed to have the full authority of God during His ministry. His miracles certainly provide further evidence that Jesus had the potential to reveal divine power when it served the greater goals of the kingdom. But Paul reminds us that God's ways are not our ways; that the mind of Christ may appear "upside-down" from our way of saving the world.

GROWTH ASSIGNMENT

Make a list of all the ways you know that Jesus is God. How powerful, or able is Jesus to help with the problems you may be facing? What are some of your questions or doubts about Jesus' full divinity? Spend some time inviting the Lord to help you experience that Jesus is God. Are there some specific areas into which you would like God to intervene?

Jesus Was Fully Human

> *. . . but made himself nothing, taking the very nature of a servant, being made in human likeness.*
> *Philippians 2:7 (NIV)*

Inherent in the mind of our Creator was that the world was created *"very good."* Whereas Greek philosophy sought to put the physical nature behind and aspire to a higher plane of intellectual and spiritual *"other-worldliness,"* the biblical picture of the Lord is as One who redeems His lost and undone human creatures. *God's Word* is not theoretical. When God speaks, action happens. There is no separation between what God says and what occurs. Therefore, God's plan of salvation was not one to throw away the physical world, but to redeem it by entering it Himself: heart, soul, mind, and body. The promise of God's world saving love *"put skin on"* when God became a human being in Jesus. We call this the *incarnation - putting flesh on* God's promise to save.

The influence of Handel's *Messiah* has permeated our culture's holiday celebrations with a musical memory of scriptures surrounding the incarnation. Matthew and Luke's stories about the birth of Jesus are steeped in the recognition that Jesus is the fulfillment of God's promise.

But while he (Joseph) thought about these things, behold, an angel of the Lord appeared to him in a dream, saying, "Joseph, son of David, do not be afraid to take to you Mary your wife, for that which is conceived in her is of the Holy Spirit. And she will bring forth a Son, and you shall call His name JESUS, for He will save His people from their sins. So all this was done that it might be fulfilled which was spoken by the Lord through the prophet, saying: "Behold, the virgin shall be with child, and bear a Son, and they shall call His name Immanuel," which is translated, "God with us."

Matthew 1:20-22 (NKJV)

Simeon took Him (Jesus) in his arms and praised God saying: "Sovereign Lord, as you have promised, you now dismiss your servant in peace. For my eyes have seen your salvation, which you have prepared in the sight of all people, a light for revelation to the Gentiles and for glory to your people Israel."

Luke 2:28-32 (NIV)

We know very little about the first thirty years of Jesus' life. The Scriptures make only a few references to these years. But we do know He learned the trade of Joseph, a builder from Nazareth, in Galilee. He was raised *"according to the law"* in Judaism, had remarkable insight into the things of God, and *grew in wisdom and stature, and in favor with God and men.* (Luke 2:52) These were formative years preparing Him for what lay ahead.

Before beginning ministry, Jesus exhibited humility and a deep concern to work according to the Scriptures by asking John to baptize Him in the Jordan. A voice was heard from heaven saying: *"You are my Son, whom I love; with you I am well pleased."* (Luke 3:22) John the Baptist himself gave this testimony:

> *I saw the Spirit coming down from heaven like a dove and resting upon him. I did not know him, but he who sent me to baptize in water had told me, "When you see the Spirit coming down upon someone and resting upon him, you will know that this is he who is to baptize in the Holy Spirit." I saw it myself, and I have borne witness. This is God's Chosen One.*
>
> John 1:32-34 (NEB)

Immediately Jesus was driven by the Spirit into the wilderness where He was tempted by Satan for forty days. For those who wonder whether Jesus was really human or not, the temptations of Jesus show us how the Son of God dealt with very human reality. Through His love of the Father and reliance on the Scriptures, Jesus' endurance not only overcame the deprivations of His body, but gave us a model of how to break sin's hold over us in our own temptations.

> *For we have not a high priest who is unable to sympathize with our weaknesses, but one who in every respect has been tempted as we are, yet without sin. Let us then with confidence draw near to the throne of grace, that we may receive mercy and find grace to help in time of need.*
>
> Hebrews 4:15-16 (RSV)

GROWTH ASSIGNMENT

How human was Jesus? Spend some time quietly imagining Jesus' life as a child, adolescent, adult growing up in Palestine. What are some of your own very human struggles? How would Jesus have dealt with them? What do you imagine was the hardest part of Jesus' suffering and dying for our salvation? As you contemplate what Jesus did out of love for you, what might you say to Him for His fully human example?

Jesus Came To Serve

- taking the very nature of a servant . . .
Philippians 2:7 (NIV)

One of the most difficult aspects of Jesus' ministry was that He didn't use His divine authority to force His Kingdom to come. In fact, in place of coming *"top down"* to save the world, it's as though God's whole plan was to roll up His sleeves, get beneath the needs of the world, and serve us into heaven. Even His disciples struggled with the idea that faith's strength came not from demonstrations of might, but through humble sacrifices for the benefit of others. Jesus taught that God was more concerned with the integrity of our character in secret places than through public displays of religion. He used His own life as an example that instead of seeking reputation and power over others, true greatness comes through serving:

> *You know that those who are regarded as rulers of the Gentiles lord it over them, and their high officials exercise authority over them. Not so with you. Instead, whoever wants to become great among you must be your servant, and whoever wants to be first must be slave of all. For even the Son of Man did not come to be served, but to serve, and to give his life as a ransom for many."*
> *Mark 10:42-45 (NIV)*

Once, when demonstrating what such service looked like, Jesus took off His robes and began to wash His disciples' feet. They were terribly confused.

> *He (Jesus) said to them, "Do you know what I have done to you? You call me 'Teacher' and 'Lord,' and you are right, for so I am. If I then, the Lord and the Teacher, washed your feet, you also ought to wash one another's feet. For I gave you an example that you also should do as I did to you. Truly, truly, I say to you, a slave is not greater than His master; neither is one who is sent greater than the one who sent him. If you know these*

things, you are blessed if you do them."

John 13:12-17 (NAS)

GROWTH ASSIGNMENT

How would you rate the service at your favorite restaurant? What do they do for you there that makes you feel special? What is the message conveyed through service? Spend some time asking Jesus to do in your life the service only He can provide. Is there anything you would have a difficult time allowing Jesus to do in your life? What lesson might Jesus want you to learn through His example of serving you? Is there someone you may need to serve?

Jesus Humbled Himself

> *And being found in appearance as a man, he humbled himself . . .*
>
> Philippians 2:8 (NIV)

Each Christmas we are brought to ponder the unfathomable - the Son of God came to earth, not in a palace, but in a barn. On Good Friday we are amazed over and over again that the only truly Righteous/Sinless One was crucified - and for our sins! One of the key characteristics of the ministry of Jesus is that He didn't have to flaunt Himself. No great noise, no media spin, Jesus came just as He was. He spoke the truth in love in the hopes of drawing people from sin into the kingdom of God. He performed miracles and often told recipients not to tell anyone, because His goal was to point them to a living relationship with the Lord. He called people, not to jump on a bandwagon, but to weigh carefully the cost of following Jesus - advice which led many to walk away.

Humility is not worthlessness. Rather, humility is being what you truly are, *"of the earth."* Jesus did not call people to pride, prestige, or hypocrisy (acting under a false identity), but rather, for people to come to God genuinely, just as they were. He lived the truth of what James said:

> *Humble yourselves in the sight of the Lord, and He shall lift you up.*
>
> James 4:10 (KJV)

The self-giving act of *"emptying Himself"* for our salvation was motivated by pure compassion. It was the undying love of God that understood the fragile nature of His broken creatures that caused Him to live in lowliness and do whatever it took to restore lost souls to wholeness of heart, soul, mind, and strength.

> *He will feed his flock like a shepherd, he will gather the lambs in his arms, he will carry them in his bosom, and gently lead those that are with young.*
>
> Isaiah 40:11 (RSV)

Without humility it is impossible to grasp the heart of Jesus' teachings. Truly humble people have nothing to prove. When accused of crimes He did not commit, in humility, *"Jesus remained silent and gave no answer."* (Mark 14:61) In humility Jesus did not strike back when He was mocked and beaten. In humility Jesus refrained from calling down the power of heaven while dying on the cross. In true humility He demonstrated the greatest love which was willing to lay itself down for others. Only in humility can we understand His words and discover God's power to transform an entire world.

> *Love your enemies, do good to those who hate you, bless those who curse you, pray for those who mistreat you. If someone strikes you on one cheek, turn to him the other also. If someone takes your cloak, do not stop him from taking your tunic. Give to everyone who asks you, and if anyone takes what belongs to you, do not demand it back. Do to others as you would have them do to you.*
>
> Luke 6:27-31 (NIV)

GROWTH ASSIGNMENT

When is the last time you had to admit you were wrong? What made it so difficult? What does pride do to human relationships? What does pride do with the truth? What act of Jesus' humility most touches you? Is there an act of humility you may need to demonstrate to someone?

Jesus Was The Model Of Obedience

. . . and became obedient to death . . .
Philippians 2:8 (NIV)

Jesus was the fulfillment of God's promise. Therefore, His ministry was conducted in accordance with the will and Word of God. His temptations in the wilderness were resolved through discerning God's intent in scripture. Luke records His first sermon as a quotation of Isaiah 61:1-2, summarizing Jesus' commitment to fulfill God's purpose in sending Him:

"The Spirit of the Lord is upon me, because he has anointed me to bring good news to the poor. He has sent me to proclaim release to the captives and recovery of sight to the blind, to let the oppressed go free, to proclaim the year of the Lord's favor." And he rolled up the scroll, gave it back to the attendant, and sat down. The eyes of all in the synagogue were fixed on him. Then he began to say to them, "Today this scripture has been fulfilled in your hearing."
Luke 4:18-21 (NRSV)

Jesus became known as a **Rabbi,** Hebrew for *Teacher.* But He was not like other teachers of His day. Jesus had a passion to connect common people with the heart of God. From childhood He had been raised according to the teachings of the Old Testament. But He didn't teach *"Law."* Many of Jesus' instructions were in story form, called *parables,* to help paint word pictures that might explain the deep things of God to the people. Jesus' teaching style was very popular with the common folk of His day. Religious leaders, however, found Him troublesome. They were deeply suspicious that He was operating outside the Law of Moses. To reassure them, Jesus said:

"Do not suppose that I have come to abolish the Law and the prophets; I did not come to abolish, but to complete. I tell you this: so long as heaven and earth endure, not a

55

letter, not a stroke, will disappear from the Law until all
that must happen has happened."
Matthew 5:17-18 (NEB)

Scribes and teachers of the Law were concerned with conveying the *letter of the Law.* They sought compliance to what the Law said. Jesus used what the Law said as a doorway to learn the *spirit of the Law,* and thus, get to know the author (God). Jesus spent a great deal of time going past the actions of those who complied with the Law's letter and missed its meaning. For example, Jesus told the story of the Good Samaritan (Luke 10:25-37) to an expert in the Law who was testing Jesus on how to inherit eternal life. They both agreed that the key to eternal life is:

You shall love the LORD your God with all your heart,
with all your soul, with all your strength, and with all
you mind; and your neighbor as yourself.
Luke 10:27 (NKJV)

But the man wanted to justify himself, so He asked Jesus, *"And who is my neighbor?"* Jesus then told the story about a priest, a Levite (Temple and worship caretaker), and a Samaritan (despised by Jews). The first two passed by a man beaten half to death along the road. They were both "right" according to the Law not to touch the injured man so they wouldn't become "unclean." But the Samaritan picked up the hurt man and took care of him. Jesus concluded by asking who really did God's will and was a neighbor?

And he said, "He who showed mercy on him." Then Jesus
said to him, "Go and do likewise."
Luke 10:37 (NKJV)

Jesus was not satisfied only bringing people to the Law. He wanted to bring them to God. He came to accomplish the will of the Father. Jesus modeled obedience to God's will in His own temptations. He demonstrated how to arrive at obedience in His prayers and ministry. The greatest example of obedience is Jesus' prayer in Gethsemane.

He withdrew about a stone's throw beyond them, knelt down and prayed, "Father, if you are willing, take this cup from me; yet not my will, but yours be done." An angel from heaven appeared to him and strengthened him. And being in anguish, he prayed more earnestly, and his sweat was like drops of blood falling to the ground.

Luke 22:41-44 (NIV)

Jesus made obedience to the person of God central to His disciples' instructions. He even sent them into the world to teach others the same.

All authority in heaven and on earth has been given to me. Go therefore and make disciples of all nations, baptizing them in the name of the Father and of the Son and of the Holy Spirit, teaching them to observe all that I have commanded you; and lo, I am with you always, to the close of the age.

Matthew 28:18-20 (RSV)

Obedience runs contrary to the human will. But through the discipline of setting personal agendas and ambitions aside, Jesus calls us to practice doing what does not come naturally - seeking and doing God's will. In obedience, we can lay aside our selfish standards and commit to live by the highest standards for the highest good. Jesus' one commandment is both simple and will take the rest of our lives.

I give you a new commandment, that you love one another. Just as I have loved you, you also should love one another. By this everyone will know that you are my disciples, if you have love for one another.

John 13:34-35 (NRSV)

Is there a cup you would like to ask God to take from your hands? What do you believe God really wants you to do? Is it truly in the spirit of His will? What will it cost you if you say yes? What will it cost you if you say no? What would have happened if Jesus had said no to God's will? In ten thousand years what will you wish you had done? What kind of help has God put around you to encourage you? What will you do?

Jesus Suffered For What Was Right

. . . even death on a cross!

Philippians 2:8 (NIV)

Jesus taught that falling in love with the things of God comes with a price. Those who would follow Him were cautioned about the cost of being a disciple. Simply living to seek what God wants risks our relationships, comfort, health, predictability, even safety. While one of the greatest human fears is pain, Jesus showed through His ministry how to see beyond pain to the greater glory of God. Isaiah foresaw that the Messiah would be a suffering servant.

> *But He was pierced through for our transgressions, He was crushed for our iniquities; The chastening for our well-being fell upon Him, And by His scourging we are healed.*
>
> *Isaiah 53:5 (NAS)*

Even at the beginning of His ministry, Jesus blesses those who suffer for God as having received a greater reward.

> *Blessed are those who are persecuted because of righteousness, for theirs is the kingdom of heaven. Blessed are you when people insult you, persecute you, and falsely say all kinds of evil against you because of me. Rejoice and be glad, because great is your reward in heaven, for in the same way they persecuted the prophets who were before you.*
>
> *Matthew 5:10-12 (NIV)*

He could say this with confidence, because it was the same way He was to be treated. Jesus lived with the reality that pain and death are not the worst that can happen. In fact, our avoidance of suffering can cause us to miss the most important things.

I tell you, my friends, do not fear those who kill the body, and after that have no more that they can do. But I warn you whom to fear: fear him who, after he has killed, has the power to cast into hell; yes, I tell you fear him!
Luke 12:4-5 (RSV)

Only God can throw us into hell. Therefore, the only real fear we need have is, not suffering, but being out of relationship with God. Jesus accepted the normal human struggles that came to Him through daily living for the kingdom of God. He accepted the cost that came to Him as the Lamb of God. Immediately after His disciples recognized that Jesus was indeed the Messiah, He began to prepare them for the road ahead.

He began to teach them that the Son of Man must suffer many things and be rejected by the elders, chief priests, and teachers of the law, and that he must be killed and after three days rise again. He spoke plainly about this, and Peter took him aside and began to rebuke him. But when Jesus turned and looked at his disciples, he rebuked Peter. "Get behind me, Satan!" he said. "You do not have in mind the things of God, but the things of men."
Mark 8:31-33 (NIV)

Peter speaks for most of us who cry "No, Jesus, not the way of suffering!" But an amazing transformation took place in Peter's understanding of the role of suffering for God. In the letter 1 Peter 2, Peter advises younger Christians how to bear up under unjust suffering, even as slaves for the sake of God. He seems to have learned:

For even hereunto were ye called: because Christ also suffered for us, leaving us an example, that ye should follow His steps.

1 Peter 2:21 (KJV)

The worst suffering for Jesus came as a result of His obedience to God to bear the punishment in His sinless body that should have been ours. The cross was the ultimate shame for a Jew, not only because of the tortuous, slow death before the public eye. Old Testament Law said: *"anyone who is hung on a tree is under God's curse."* (Deuteronomy 21:23) Jesus actually became cursed as *"Guilty,"* substituting Himself for us, so the sentence intended for us could be met. In fact, by embracing the suffering that came with living for God, Jesus' suffering even unto death produced eternal benefits for us all.

And while being reviled, He did not revile in return; while suffering, He uttered no threats, but kept entrusting Himself to Him who judges righteously; and He Himself bore our sins in His body on the cross, that we might die to sin and live to righteousness; for by His wounds you were healed. For you were continually straying like sheep, but now you have returned to the Shepherd and Guardian of your souls.

1 Peter 2:23-25 (NAS)

GROWTH ASSIGNMENT

What are the ways Jesus suffered for you? What is the worst form of suffering you can imagine? Can you think of some things that are not worth suffering for? What forms of suffering might just be common to being human? What might be some things worth suffering for? We tend to ask God to deliver us from suffering. However, what might be the benefits of suffering for the right things? Are you suffering right now? What might God be suggesting to you?

Jesus Is Raised And Glorified

Therefore God exalted him to the highest place and gave him the name that is above every name, that at the name of Jesus every knee should bow, in heaven and on earth and under the earth, and every tongue confess that Jesus Christ is Lord, to the glory of God the Father.
Philippians 2:9-11 (NIV)

If Jesus had simply lived a great life of teaching and then died, we may have remembered His words as valuable wisdom. We would have thought "How sad that such a good man should die unjustly." That, in fact, and the accompanying fear that they would be next to die was the attitude of Jesus' followers in the day and a half following His crucifixion. They were hiding in fear and in despair.

Late that Sunday evening, when the disciples were together behind locked doors, for fear of the Jews . . .
John 20:19 (NEB)

Early on the third day some had come from the cemetery announcing that Jesus' grave was empty. But an empty grave did not prove anything, other than perhaps someone had stolen His body. The greatest evidence of the resurrection of Jesus is the existence of the Church! Those who knew Him best, including His own family who had ridiculed Him during His ministry saw Jesus appear, raised from the dead!

Then he said to Thomas, "Put your finger here; see my hands. Reach out your hand and put it into my side. Stop doubting and believe." Thomas said to him, "My Lord and my God!" Then Jesus told him, "Because you have seen me, you have believed; blessed are those who have not seen and yet have believed."
John 20:27-29 (NIV)

The remaining eleven disciples (Judas Iscariot had hanged himself in shame because of his betrayal of Jesus) were so changed by the experience of their *"Risen Lord"* that tradition remembers they all died taking the story of Jesus' resurrection to the ends of their known world. The resurrection validates the truth and power of God in what Jesus had said. Only in the light of His resurrection were His followers able to make full sense of what He had taught. When the women at the tomb discovered the empty grave, angels appeared to them.

> *"Why do you look for the living among the dead? He is not here, but has risen. Remember how he told you, while he was still in Galilee, that the Son of Man must be handed over to sinners, and be crucified, and on the third day rise again." Then they remembered his words . . .*
>
> Luke 24:5-8 (NRSV)

In the power of His resurrection we are invited by God into a life of daily transformation. Not only does God win us from past sin, but in Jesus, we are empowered to live wholly new in the present and future. Eternal life starts now. If the power of God is at work in us bringing life out of death, then no obstacle in our experience can keep us from living victoriously for God. We can truly be *"more than conquerors"* as Paul writes;

> *For I am sure that neither death, nor life, nor angels, nor principalities, nor things present, nor things to come, nor powers, nor height, nor depth, nor anything else in all creation, will be able to separate us from the love of God in Christ Jesus our Lord.*
>
> Romans 8:38-39 (RSV)

Without the resurrection, the Church of Jesus is "most to be pitied." Without it, we are just another group of people doing *"good deeds."* But in the resurrection we find our place and purpose in this world. We are changed to be firstfruits of the redemption God is bringing to all creation.

What was undone by sin and death begins its renewal here and now in the transformed women and men who live to proclaim God's victorious kingdom to others. We are living advertisements of God's resuscitating power until He comes.

> *But Christ has indeed been raised from the dead, the firstfruits of those who have fallen asleep. For since death came through a man, the resurrection of the dead comes also through a man. For as in Adam all die, so in Christ all will be made alive. But each in his own turn: Christ, the firstfruits; then, when he comes, those who belong to him. Then the end will come, when he hands over the kingdom to God the Father after he has destroyed all dominion, authority and power. For he must reign until he has put all his enemies under his feet. The last enemy to be destroyed is death. For he "has put everything under his feet."*
>
> 1 Corinthians 15:20-27 (NIV)

GROWTH ASSIGNMENT

Take a few minutes to pray about your perceptions of Jesus. Would you add any other images of how you know the Savior? What aspect of Jesus' ministry do you find most helpful? Are any troubling? What questions would you ask God about sending His Son? If Jesus is truly Lord, are there any areas of your life which still lack His lordship?

Power To Do God's Work

If religious experts missed recognizing Jesus, his stunned followers knew they were even less likely to be able to carry on the proclamation of God's kingdom in Jesus' name. During that time Jesus appeared and told them to wait in Jerusalem until they received power from on high. Then they would be His *witnesses* (Greek - *martus* - *those who remember*) to the ends of the earth. His promised power would change them and enable them to remember that God changes people. In weakness and fear, they spent the days following Jesus' death and resurrection in constant prayer.

Do not leave Jerusalem, but wait for the gift my father promised, which you have heard me speak about. For John baptized with water, but in a few days, you will be baptized with the Holy Spirit.

Acts 1:4-5 (NIV)

And again in verse 8 of the same chapter,

"But you will receive power when the Holy Spirit comes on you; and you will be my witnesses in Jerusalem, and in all Judea and Samaria, and to the ends of the earth."

Acts 1:8 (NIV)

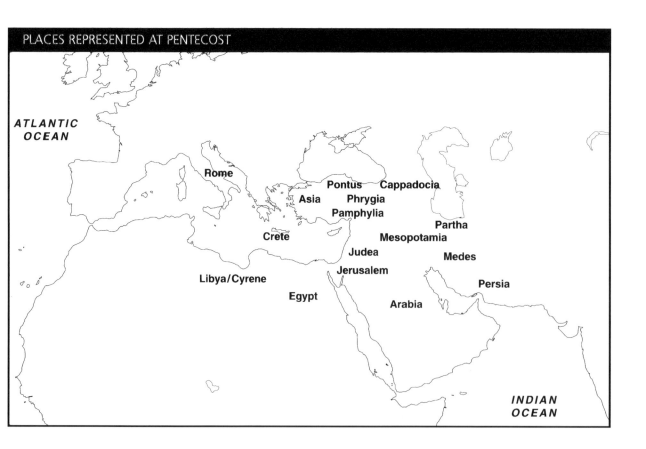

PLACES REPRESENTED AT PENTECOST

As you look forward to a life of serving Jesus, what personal gifts do you bring to offer to God? Are there any specific areas where your personal inadequacies cause confusion or fear in your future?

On the day of Pentecost, the fiftieth day after the Sabbath of Passover week, the followers of Jesus, common, ordinary people, were gathered together and God changed them.

> *And suddenly there came from heaven a noise like a violent, rushing wind, and it filled the whole house where they were sitting. And there appeared to them tongues as of fire distributing themselves, and they rested on each one of them. And they were all filled with the Holy Spirit and began to speak with other tongues, as the Spirit was giving them utterance.*
>
> *Acts 2:2-4 (NAS)*

Jesus' followers were not the only ones in Jerusalem during Passover. Tens of thousands of Jewish pilgrims who had come to celebrate the festival from every point of the compass heard the Gospel in their own language. They were so touched that 3,000 accepted Jesus as Lord and Savior and became believers in that early church. Instantly, the Church of Jesus Christ became an international body of believers. As these young Christians returned to their homes in Rome, in Egypt, in Arabia, in Mesopotamia, in Crete, and in North Africa, they carried the Gospel with them.

We cannot accomplish the work of God, unless the Lord helps us. The power to spread the news of Jesus does not rest on his believers but on God Himself. Sharing Jesus always begins right where we are (in Jerusalem), and moves with us as we go into the world. As you read this, are there people you know who might benefit from what you are learning about God? What might you do to move toward sharing the Good News of what God is doing in your life?

Chapter Four

THE FOLLOWERS OF JESUS

New Religion Or Completion Of The Old

THE FIRST CHRISTIANS DID NOT SEE themselves as starting a new religion. It is important to remember that the earliest Christians were primarily Jewish people who had found their Messiah in Jesus Christ. This led to some difficulty in relation to other Jewish movements. The Pharisees, for example, were committed to a genuinely well-intentioned goal to bring Jewish people into compliance with the laws of the Old Testament as the means of becoming right with God. Pharisees felt that the early Christians were misunderstanding the scriptures: Jesus could not have been their Messiah.

The Conversion Of An Enemy Of Jesus

Saul, a leader among Pharisees, committed himself to stamp out the Christian movement. On his way to Damascus to root out believers there, God miraculously introduced Saul to Jesus in a blinding light. His conversion so changed his life that his name changed to Paul. He felt God had changed him in order to carry the Gospel not only to Jews, but also especially to non-Jews, or *Gentiles*.

Paul's mission adventures came about as he traveled from town to town telling people about Jesus. Typically, Paul began by teaching about Jesus in the local synagogue. Then, when Jewish leaders threw him out, he would preach to the *Gentile* population. Small Christian churches were planted in many of the places he preached. The majority of the New Testament is a collection of letters Paul wrote advising these young congregations how to live for Jesus.

GROWTH ASSIGNMENT

If you look at the maps in the back of your Bible, you should find one that shows the places Paul visited. Can you find the names of towns that received New Testament letters?

Paul tried to teach the members of these churches how to live together as one body despite great differences among them. He hoped to teach them to live faithfully in a world that was often hostile to the message of Jesus. Roman rule dictated that worship of the emperor and the Roman pantheon of many gods was the official religion of the empire. Judaism, however, was generally tolerated during the early years of the Christian church, possibly because Jewish adherents were so numerous in the Roman Empire (as many as 15%), and because previous attempts to enforce emperor worship on Jewish peoples had led to violent revolt. Until about 70 A.D., Christianity was considered a part of Judaism.

Tension Mounts

But even within the Church, as more Gentiles became followers of Christ, tension mounted over whether non-Jewish believers needed to adhere to the Jewish law in order to be bona-fide Christians. The matter was settled in a pivotal meeting in Jerusalem. After listening to all sides in the argument, James, the brother of Jesus, who was the leader of the Church at the time, decided:

We should not make it difficult for the Gentiles who are turning to God. Instead, we should write to them, telling them to abstain from food polluted by idols, from sexual immorality, from the meat of strangled animals and from blood.

Acts 15:19-20 (NIV)

This, however, led to greater strain with non-Christian Jewish leaders who were already skeptical of the *"Jesus of Nazareth movement."* In 70 A.D., two very significant things happened to change the status of Christianity with regard to Judaism. The first was that leaders of the Jewish faith in Jerusalem officially declared that Christianity was not Jewish. Secondly, in order to put an end to uprisings of Jewish nationalism, the Roman government sent its armies to destroy Jerusalem and the Temple. The young Christian Church was scattered to the wind - where it continued to grow. It was in Antioch that they were first called *Christians.*

Correcting False Teaching

As the Christian Church spread to more and more lands, encounters with ideologies contrary to the teachings of Jesus grew too. The risk of *false teaching,* or **heresy,** creeping into the Church became even greater as those who knew Jesus personally died. It became important for church leaders to clarify what was acceptable Christian belief. In order to curtail the risk of changing the intent of Jesus' teaching over time, regional Church leaders gathered for *councils* to discuss key points of faith. The conclusions of these early councils were statements of faith called *creeds, from the Latin word, "credo," for "I believe."* Each creed sought to summarize, in a succinct fashion, key and orthodox Christian understanding. ***The Apostles' Creed, Athanasian Creed, and Nicene Creed*** are examples of early church statements of faith. Here follows a copy of the Nicene Creed:

We believe in one God, the Father, the Almighty,
Maker of heaven and earth, of all that is, seen and unseen.
We believe in one Lord, Jesus Christ, the only Son of God,
eternally begotten of the Father, God from God,
Light from Light, true God from true God,
begotten, not made, of one Being with the Father;
through Him all things were made.

For us and for our salvation He came down from heaven,
was incarnate of the Holy Spirit and the Virgin Mary
and became truly human.

For our sake He was crucified under Pontius Pilate;
He suffered death and was buried. On the third day
He rose again in accordance with the Scriptures;
He ascended into heaven and is seated at the right hand
of the Father. He will come again in glory to judge the living
and the dead, and His kingdom will have no end.

We believe in the Holy Spirit, the Lord, the giver of life,
who proceeds from the Father, who with the Father and the Son
is worshiped and glorified, who has spoken through the prophets.
We believe in one holy Christian* and apostolic church.
We acknowledge one baptism for the forgiveness of sins.
We look for the resurrection of the dead, and the
life of the world to come. Amen.

*Ancient text reads "catholic," which means "universal."
English text as used in the Moravian Book of Worship. Prepared by the
English Language Liturgical Consultation (ELLC), 1988.

GROWTH ASSIGNMENT

Compose your own credo. What key points of faith would you be sure to address? Can you identify from the Nicene Creed some matters of faith that may have needed clarification?

The Emperor Becomes A Christian

During the first centuries of Christianity, there were no church buildings. For the most part, congregations continued their witness quietly, only periodically suffering the suspicion of government officials because of their secretive ways. People met in homes, tombs, or other places of hiding, and when possible, in public settings such as bathhouses for their worship celebrations. In 313 A.D., however, the hidden nature of Christianity changed dramatically when the Roman Emperor, **Constantine**, accepted Christ as his Lord and Savior and became a Christian. Imagine the trauma to the Church when in the course of his lifetime, Constantine sought to transform Christianity from being an illegal religion to the official religion of the Roman Empire.

While the exterior of the Roman world took on a Christian veneer, under the surface the Church found itself absorbing pagan practice, ideology, and people. Formerly pagan priests that were quite unfamiliar with the Christian faith found themselves leading churches. Our celebration of the birth of Jesus on December 25th stems from this time. Prior to Constantine's conversion, Christians didn't really celebrate the birth of Jesus. However, Romans had celebrated the birth of the sun god on December 25th. Constantine knew that this pagan practice should not continue, and since the date of Jesus' birth is not mentioned in Scripture, Roman Christianity substituted the birth of Jesus for the sun god.

A more substantial change took place in the shift of power within the Christian church. Where previously leaders of churches regionally shared a similar measure of power and influence in decision making around the Mediterranean, now the leader of the Church of Rome had the Emperor as one of his constituents. Therefore, the position of the Church in Rome took on a greatly expanded role and influence in comparison to the leaders in other areas of the Christian Church. The Church in Rome inherited a very military style of decision-making and communication. Roman-centric power went from the top to the bottom. Roman Christians shifted away from Greek-based scripture by translating the New Testament into Latin. This **vulgate** or *common tongue* translation would serve western Christian practice for the next thousand years.

Holy Wars

When the western half of the Roman Empire fell to invaders in the 400's, Europe began to disintegrate into the feudalism of the Dark Ages. The western Church was left holding incredible power. This elevated position and practice of Roman church leaders added to traditional tensions with non-Roman centers of Christian faith. A schism between eastern and western Christianity gradually developed over centuries. By the Middle Ages the friction became so great that the one Christian Church was more formally divided into western and eastern halves. *Roman Catholicism* viewed itself as the *universal church*. *Eastern Orthodoxy* saw itself as the *right way* of Christianity.

During the disaffection between eastern and western Christians, a middle-eastern man named *Muhammad* began a search for the way to God. Disillusioned with Judaism and Christianity, he retreated to the deserts of Arabia. There, he claimed to receive revelations from God, which completed what the teachings of the Old Testament and Jesus had left undone. He wrote of his revelations in the *Qur'an*. His followers spread the message of Islam across Arabia into Palestine, through northern Africa into Spain, and around Asia Minor to southern Europe in what is today Albania, Croatia, and Bosnia. As the Islamic armies came to a town, those who would accept the new faith became Muslim and those who refused the new faith were often killed. The "People of the Book" (Jews and Christians), however, were allowed to keep and practice their faiths as long as they paid tribute to Islam and did not seek to make converts. In fact, many Christians in North Africa and elewhere, disillusioned by the doctrinal and political controversies within Christendom, voluntarily converted to the new religion. Through this fashion, by the 700's, *Islam* was approaching the very heart of Europe itself.

In response, the *Pope* (Italian *Papa - Father*) of the Church in Rome searched throughout feudal Europe for someone militarily strong enough to unite Europe to stanch the spread of *Islam*. He found in the person of *King Charles*

Martel, such a man. Martel defeated the Islamic forces in 732 A.D. at Tours. Seventy years later, on Christmas Day, 800 A.D., Charles Martel's grandson, *Charlemagne,* was crowned *Holy Roman Emperor* by the Pope in an effort to further unite Europe. It was hoped this act would bring together both the spiritual and political realms of Europe under a unified front. As a result, the Church came into a new measure of influence. Now, in order to rule the people, the Emperor needed the blessing of the Church. The next centuries saw a series of military campaigns called "crusades," theoretically intended to wrest the "Holy Land" from the hand of Muslim forces. European nobility expended much effort in the name of religion which was often driven by political, personal, or financial ambition more than matters of true faith.

GROWTH ASSIGNMENT

What values of faith do you hold over which you would not compromise? What areas of faith do you believe require the ability to "celebrate differences?" When does what others believe separate them outside of "the faith?" Who could you pray for today that thinks differently from you?

Meanwhile, In Central Europe

In the ninth and tenth centuries, the Greek Orthodox Church sent missionaries Cyril and Methodius to bring the Gospel to the tribes of central Europe. Under the influence of Cyril and Methodius, the Czech and Slovak peoples accepted Christ and an indigenous church began. Cyril is responsible for having developed a written alphabet that bears his name and is still used in parts of Eastern Europe.

However, as the Holy Roman Empire expanded, Czech churches eventually came under Rome's influence as well. Seeds of reform were planted as the indigenous expression of Czech faith and worship was supplanted by Rome-centered activity. This period of history is known as the Middle or Dark Ages because so few people could read or write. The Roman Church actually increased its power by controlling the information of reading and writing. Those who wanted to learn needed to go to the Church. Those who wanted to rule politically also needed the blessing of the Church. Thus, church leaders wielded incredible influence over the lives of nearly everyone. The sentiment began to arise that the Church was more concerned with maintaining its power than in the will and word of God.

Change Is In The Wind

Europeans were still reeling from the decimation of "the Plague" in the mid 14th century. The "Black Death" had killed one third of the population and caused people to re-think many things. In England, John Wycliffe began translating the Latin *Vulgate* into English. His attempt to reform the practice of faith by basing it in the culture and language of the English people was met with a quick reprisal from Rome. John Wycliffe was imprisoned and his work destroyed. But on the other side of Europe, in Prague, Wycliffe's ideas had stimulated great interest. Nationalist fervor there, coupled with desires to reform the Church, led to the establishment of a preaching chapel specifically to allow for Czech to be the language of worship and teaching. John Hus, Roman Catholic priest, professor at the University of Prague, and gifted speaker, became a sort of spokesperson for the reform movement.

Increased Participation In Worship

Among Hus' reforms, opportunities for believers to participate personally in worship were explored. Previously, the clergy had, in a sense, performed worship for the Church. Participants in communion were only permitted the bread; priests alone could drink the cup of Christ's sacrificed blood. Professional choirs typically sang the hymns of worship. Now, under Hus, hymn singing became a standard part of church life. Hymn verses were written on the whitewashed walls of the building to teach the congregation songs of praise. Both the bread and the cup began to be offered in communion to all believers.

John Hus

Understanding The Bible

In addition to putting preaching and worship in the language of the people, these church leaders in Prague translated the scriptures into Czech. They believed each person should be able to have access to the Word of God directly if they were to be obedient to the teachings of Jesus. Instruction in reading and writing made education for all believers a high priority in the Church's work. The reformers believed that Scripture alone was the standard for practice and belief of Christianity, not the traditions or hierarchy of the Church. Hus was vocal that when compared to the teachings of the Bible, clergy were corrupt and immoral and in need of repentance. This was a direct affront to the position of power that the Roman Church's leadership had enjoyed.

No To Indulgences

The Czech reformers also spoke against the sale of *indulgences.* During the Middle Ages, it was perceived that when Christians sinned, they were in danger of going to *purgatory* after they died. *Purgatory* was thought to be a sort of prison for Christians before entering Heaven. If a penitent person were to go to the priest, the repentant person could pay a fee or perform a service to the Church and receive an *indulgence* that would remit some or all of the anticipated punishment in purgatory. The Church used some of these funds and people's service to support the later Crusades. Much of the wealth went into the coffers of church leaders. John Hus denounced the whole theory of indulgences as un-biblical and as further evidence of corruption among clergy.

As a result of the changes taking place in the Church in Prague, Roman Catholic leaders invited Hus to the Council of Constance under the pretense of simply discussing his ideas for reform. However, after a mock trial and imprisonment, he was declared a heretic, defrocked, and burned at the stake on July 6, 1415. Meanwhile, his followers back in Prague committed themselves to continue Hus' teachings. Bitter bloodshed broke out when the Holy Roman Empire's armies moved into the Czech lands to put down the reform movement. A confusing time ensued in which Czech nationals joined forces with church reformers to fight a bitter war lasting decades.

Amidst the hostilities, a small group of Hus' followers retreated to the Valley of Kunwald, where they refused to

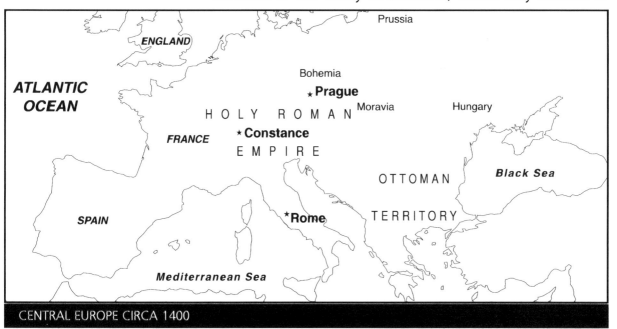

CENTRAL EUROPE CIRCA 1400

have any further part in committing bloodshed for the sake of church transformation. In good conscience, however, they felt the Roman Church would not be open to change. Therefore, in 1457, they determined to begin a new body called the **Unity of the Brethren** (*Latin: Unitas Fratrum*). They began a search for the ideal Christian community that they hoped was preserved somewhere in the world. Schools were opened to teach men and women, young and old, to read. Congregations were begun, and pastors and church leaders were selected to provide leadership.

As the 16th century began, the winds of change had blown across the rest of Europe. In 1515, a Roman Catholic priest named Martin Luther nailed 95 **protests** to the Roman religious practice on the door of his church. Hence, the **Protestant Reformation** got its beginning. The pre-

Reformation movement of the **Unity of the Brethren** was isolated a hundred years earlier by the armies of the Holy Roman Empire. Luther, however, had worked with other reform leaders throughout northern and central Europe, who shared mutual concerns. They had a better-organized political and military resistance against the Roman Catholic reactions to their reforms. When the Emperor actually sent his armies north to bring the "Protestants" back into line, Protestant armies were able to fight them to a stalemate. This is evident even to this day where parts of northern Europe are heavily Protestant and southern Europe is predominantly Roman Catholic.

The followers of Martin Luther clearly became the *Lutherans.* Those who followed John Calvin became known as *Presbyterians and others.* Zwingli's followers were the *Reformed Church.* French reformers were called *Huguenots.* The Church in England at this time was going through changes of its own. Protestant sentiment ran high in Great Britain. In addition to the theological and doctrinal tension, there were also political and economic reasons influencing the English crown to lean away from Rome. But the break didn't formally occur until King Henry VIII was excommunicated from the Roman Catholic Church for divorcing his wife. In response to his excommunication, he turned to the Archbishop of Canterbury and appointed him to direct the formation of the new *Church of England (Anglican or Episcopal).*

There were also reformers who felt as though the *Protestant Reformation* didn't go far enough to reclaim the biblical foundation of Christian faith. Some felt that since the scriptures say: *whoever believes and is baptized will be saved* (Mark 16:16) that the reformers had compromised the move back to *scripture alone* being our basis of doctrine, practice, and belief by allowing infant baptism to continue. In a kind of "reform to the reform movement," the **Anabaptists** began *re-baptizing* adult believers. They believed that only those who had made adult profession of faith should be baptized. *Mennonites, Amish, Hutterites,* and *Puritan* movements in England and subsequently *Baptists,* look to this time for their beginnings.

John Amos Comenius

In the 1500's the Unity experienced alternating periods of persecution and toleration, even receiving formal freedom from the King from 1606-1621. However, Roman Catholic powers resumed persecution of the *Unity of the Brethren* at the start of the Thirty Years War, destroying their churches, burning their schools, and driving the church into hiding. Beginning in the 1620's, the *Unity* (short form of *Unity of the Brethren*) endured a time of incredible hardship called *the hidden seed*. Families met and worshiped in secret to preserve the faith that had been passed down through generations in order to live in a simple biblical relationship with Jesus and one another. Whole settlements were uprooted to avoid prison, or worse. At points life was so bleak for the remnant of *Brethren* (another short name for the *Unity of the Brethren*) refugees that one bishop nearly single-handedly supported them through the sale of his books.

In the 1600's, *John Amos Comenius* was renowned internationally for his theories of education. The idea of putting pictures along with the text in children's books was his innovation to make learning more interesting. Comenius taught that God reveals Himself in all of life and, therefore, any study or scientific pursuit that seeks to understand God better through His creation is a worthy pursuit.

GROWTH ASSIGNMENT

What is it about the Church that you find most helpful in your relationship with God? Is there anything about the way the Church is that hinders your faith? Who are some of the people most formative in your faith? What was it about them that helped you?

Help From The Count

In 1720 a group of Moravian Brethren approached a German Lutheran nobleman by the name of *Count Nicholas Ludwig von Zinzendorf.* They told him of the plight of those who had suffered so much to maintain the purity of their faith. Stirred in his heart by their noble example, he sent word with an offer that if they were able to cross the mountains from their country to his, he would provide them asylum on his land. In 1722 the first refugees began to arrive on his estate in southeastern Germany. They began construction on the village of *Herrnhut,* which means *The Lord's Watch.* It was their intention to be a model Christian community. Over the next five years several hundred refugees as well as a variety of disillusioned Christians from different parts of Europe collected together.

Count Nicholas Ludwig von Zinzendorf

Work Only God Can Do

Herrnhut was anything but a perfect Christian community. By May, 1727, there was such animosity and bitterness amongst the settlers that the Count intervened, calling for a special meeting at his estate. After spending the night in prayer, discussion, and scripture study Zinzendorf presented them with a very basic **Brotherly Agreement** (today called *The Covenant For Christian Living*) of how Christians ought to live together.

Throughout May, June, and July, as small groups, pairs, and individuals, the community sought Biblical guidance and prayed together earnestly for God's Spirit to work in their midst.

They were hungry for God's Spirit to move among them when, on August 13th, a Communion service was held at the Berthelsdorf church, a mile from their village. As the sacrament was shared, they felt the presence of Christ and the marvel of His love and forgiveness. Old bitterness, hard words, and the anger some had felt toward each other were washed away – for many of them in a flood of tears. Hearts were opened in confession and prayer. As one of them would later write, *"On that day, we learned to love each other."*

This experience of the empowering of the Holy Spirit is often called the Birthday of the Renewed Moravian Church. The outpouring of God overflowed the residents of Herrnhut into the development of new "traditions" expressive of our faith in Christ, the phenomenal creation of a musical heritage of hymnody, anthems, and instrumental music that would be brought to Colonial America, and the ecumenical sharing of faith wherever God led them.

79

Learning To Pray

Following that August 13th experience of the Holy Spirit, prayer became the hallmark of life in Herrnhut. A group of single sisters and a group of brothers committed to pray an hour each in rotation 24 hours a day, seven days a week in support of what God was doing in and through the church. This prayer session lasted unbroken for over a hundred years. Requests began to pour in to Herrnhut for its members to travel to share what God could do in other churches if people sought the Lord. Teams from Herrnhut began visiting other churches throughout Europe bringing the spark of revival to cold, dead congregations.

Learning To Share The Gospel With Everyone

In 1731, a slave by the name of Anthony came to Herrnhut from the royal court in Denmark.

He shared with them how his own family in the West Indies did not know about Jesus. However, in order to get near enough to them, missionaries would have to become slaves themselves. Two men responded to the call. The perception was growing in Herrnhut that God had not visited them for their own blessing alone. Rather, the suffering endured during their own persecution in Moravia and Bohemia had uniquely prepared them to take the Gospel to people no one else would visit. After a year of preparation and planning, the church sent the first two missionaries to Saint Thomas in the Virgin Islands in 1732. The missionaries worked at odd jobs in order to serve and minister to the slaves who had been brought from Africa to work the sugar cane fields and plantations of the island. During the next fifty years, nearly one in three members of the Herrnhut congregation would go somewhere in the world to share the Gospel.

So passionate was their love for the Savior that missionaries from this changed congregation carried the Good News of Jesus to every inhabited continent. They were so moved by the price Jesus had paid for the salvation of the world, Moravian missionaries intentionally sought out overlooked, unreached, despised, and marginalized people to "win for the Lamb the reward of His suffering."

In 1735, a group left to establish a mission outpost in Georgia to the Native Americans and to work among newly arriving settlers. On board the ship was a young Anglican priest by the name of John Wesley and his brother, Charles. During a violent storm at sea, they had their first contact with 35 Moravians from Germany – men, women, and children going to the New World. John was terrified when a mighty wave split the mainsail and threatened to swallow the little ship. While others were screaming, the Moravians calmly sang their hymns of faith. John's diary of this experience says:

> *"I asked one of them afterward, 'Were you not afraid?' he answered, 'I thank God, no!' I asked, 'But were not your women and children afraid?' He replied, 'Our women and children are not afraid to die.'"*

Returning to England two years later, John felt himself to be a miserable failure in preaching to the American Indians. But God had plans for him (and Charles) in London. After John met the newly ordained Moravian, Peter Boehler, who was awaiting passage to Georgia, the two men walked the streets of London in animated conversation in Latin. Still struggling, John asked, *"How can I continue preaching when I do not believe that I myself am saved?"* Boehler's words would be remembered always, *"Preach faith until you have it; and then because you have it, you will preach faith."*

On May 24, 1738, still searching and unsettled, John attended a simple worship, Bible study, and prayer meeting of a small group of Moravians at Fetter Lane on Aldersgate Street in London. While the leader was reading from the Preface to the Epistle to the Romans, describing the change which God works in the heart through faith in Christ, John later wrote, *"I felt my heart strangely warmed. I felt I did trust in Christ, Christ alone for salvation."*

John Wesley pointed to this experience as his conversion. The Methodist church attributes a significant portion of its

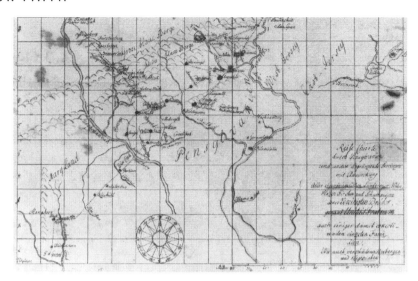

An early map of Moravian movements in America.

beginnings to the spiritual awakenings of John Wesley and his brother Charles with the Moravians. Some Pentecostal and Charismatic churches trace their beginning through this *"spiritual awakening."*

As the Moravian mission ventures and renewal work in Europe grew, the job of serving as *Chief Elder,* or leader, of the whole church became too great. Leonard Dober, who served as Chief Elder at the time, requested to be relieved of such duties. It was during the Synod meeting in London, 1741, that church leaders reached the decision that only Jesus could serve to be Chief Elder of the church. Administrators and regional leadership developed, but Moravians would have no human "Head" as other churches. They chose to rely on the Savior for direction overall. At times, they used *"the Lot"* to provide the Lord's answers to their specific questions. Usually, Scripture verses were used - one positive, one negative, and one neutral. After careful prayer and discussion, the group agreed to abide by the Lot's result as God's guidance.

No, let us speak the truth in love; so shall we fully grow up into Christ. He is the head, and on him the whole body depends. Bonded and knit together by every constituent joint, the whole frame grows through the due activity of each part, and builds itself up in love.

Ephesians 4:15-16 (NEB)

In addition to work among unreached peoples, Moravian missionaries also ministered to settlers as they moved into the New World. In Pennsylvania, away from the influence of state churches in Europe, Zinzendorf hoped to create a collegial association of churches. Recognizing that each particular *"denomination"* had a unique character and design that was helpful for reaching certain peoples, Zinzendorf attempted to develop an *"ecumenical"* council of churches. His attempts were not very successful, but do serve to point out the desire within Moravians that Christians present a common witness to the world. Moravians have been at the fore of many efforts to bring Christians together over the centuries and continue to explore ways the Body of Christ can fulfill Jesus' prayer:

> *I do not pray for these alone, but also for those who will believe in Me through their word; "That they all may be one, as You, Father, are in Me, and I in You; that they also be one in Us, that the world may believe that You sent Me. And the glory which You gave Me I have given them, that they may be one just as We are one: I in them, and You in Me; that they may be made perfect in one, and that the world may know that You sent Me, and have loved them as You have loved Me.*
>
> *John 17:20-23 (NKJV)*

Many wonder why the Moravian Church is so small if they have been around so long. Part of the reason lies in the fact that the church never went into the world to make *Moravians*. The Unity of the Brethren does not claim to be the only true Church. Rather, its members are to strive to be members of the only true Church - the Church of Jesus. Therefore, denominational loyalty has not been a motivation for evangelism. We share the love of Jesus because Jesus told us to, and because people need to know His love. It is just as joyful for someone to receive Christ and join another church as our own. Much Moravian mission work was turned over to other churches so as not to compete in the work for souls.

GROWTH ASSIGNMENT

The local congregation you attend can trace its beginnings to the spiritual awakening God did in Herrnhut. Ask your pastor or leader to share how the local congregation came to be from these beginnings.

GROWTH ASSIGNMENT

How would you compare the condition of the Church today with what you have read through its history? What does the Church today most need from the Lord? Where in the world do you see that people are not hearing the story of Jesus? Could it be that God is calling you to share the Good News in an unlikely place, that others too might live? Who could you begin by asking the Lord Jesus to awaken?

Chapter Five

The Heart Of The Church's Faith

The Ground Of Our Unity

WHEN PEOPLE IN NORTH AMERICA ASK what someone believes, we usually think in terms of personal opinion. Biblically, the concept of belief is not so much what a person thinks, but more what a person does in living. The writer of James asks a question about true faith:

> *"What good is it, my brothers and sisters, if you say you have faith but do not have works? Can faith save you?"... "So faith by itself, if it has no works, is dead."*
> *James 2:14 & 17 (NRSV)*

Faith Begins With God

In the Bible, people of faith are those willing to live as though what they say they believe is true. At the heart of the Christian faith is a necessary confidence in God. It is God's idea that we live in an eternal relationship of love with Him. God not only made us, but He made us with the intention to bless us so that we could be a blessing to others. It was God's idea to call His Church into being, to be with Him and for Him in all we think, say, or do. It is God who reveals Himself to us in His Word made flesh in

Jesus. It is the infinite God who teaches finite human beings about Himself by His Spirit. Yet, it is our confession that when we attempt to express what we truly believe about God, we put into human words and speech that which is beyond our ability to do, unless God helps us. The writer of Hebrews defines faith:

> *Now faith is the assurance of things hoped for, the conviction of things not seen.*
>
> *Hebrews 11:1 (RSV)*

Arriving at such a trust in God is more than we can achieve. Moravians attempt to describe how we are called and come to live by faith as a world Unity:

> *The Lord Jesus Christ calls His Church into being so that it may serve Him on earth until He comes. The Unitas Fratrum (Unity of the Brethren) is, therefore, aware of its being called in faith to serve humanity by proclaiming the Gospel of Jesus Christ. It recognizes this call to be the source of its being and the inspiration of its service. As is the source, so is the name and end of its being based upon the will of its Lord.*
>
> *(Ground of the Unity, paragraph 1)*

Faith Centered On The Person Of God

The Bible is very clear that we have only one God. Moses gives this admonition to all Israel:

> *"Hear, O Israel! The Lord is our God, the Lord is one! And you shall love the Lord your God with all your heart and with all your soul and with all your might."*
>
> *Deuteronomy 6:4-5 (NAS)*

There is but one God, yet there are many words and names used to describe how we know God. In the New Testament, for example, Jesus Christ and the Holy Spirit are described in ways that are truly divine. The early church, seeking to understand how this can be, taught that God is

Trinity - One God in three persons. The primary way Moravians talk about God is as Father, Son, and Holy Spirit.

> *But when he, the Spirit of truth, comes, he will guide you into all truth. He will not speak on his own; he will speak only what he hears, and he will tell you what is yet to come. He will bring glory to me by taking from what is mine and making it known to you. All that belongs to the Father is mine. That is why I said the Spirit will take from what is mine and make it known to you.*
>
> John 16:13-15 (NIV)

Many attempts to explain the *Trinity* have been made, such as that of 5th century A.D. Bishop of Hippo, Augustine. He explained the *Three in One* this way: The *Father* is like the sun; the *Son* is like the light from the sun; the *Holy Spirit* is like the heat from the sun. The three are not identical, but neither could they be separated from one another. This analogy, like all rational efforts to explain the Trinity, comes up short, because human beings can never fully comprehend the mystery of God's existence, which is unlike anything else. Nevertheless, the **doctrine** *(teaching)* of the Trinity remains central to the Christian faith because it makes the best sense out of clear biblical teachings that God is One **"and"** has revealed Himself as Father, Son, and Holy Spirit.

We know God as **Father** when we recognize the Creator and Sustainer of all the universe. We speak of the **Son** in the man Jesus, where God's promise of love became flesh to live among us, to teach us, to die for our sins, and to be raised again for our future hope of life forever. We believe that if we do not know Jesus as our Lord and Savior, if we have not experienced the benefit of His person in our lives, we cannot be assured of an eternal and saved relationship with God. It is humanly impossible to know God completely, but the person of Jesus gives us the experience of God that is enough to last forever. It is Jesus, as John says, who lets us know God:

No one has ever seen God, but God the One and Only,
who is at the Father's side, has made him known.

John 1:18 (NIV)

We know God as **Holy Spirit** when the *breath, wind, or force* of God gives us power, ability, and understanding we don't have, to be able to accomplish His purposes and experience intimate fellowship with Him and the community of faith.

When we speak of God as *Triune God*, or *Three-In-One*, we are describing God's revelation of Himself to us as the core of our belief. Remember the first question asked to those making profession of faith in Moravian churches? The question comes from this essential relationship with the Lord:

Do you believe in God as your Creator and loving heavenly
Father, in Jesus Christ as your Savior and Lord, and in the
Holy Spirit as your Comforter and Sustainer, according to
the Holy Scriptures?

(Moravian Book of Worship, page 170)

Faith Based On His Word

Moravians believe that God is present with us in the Word and the *sacraments* of baptism and communion. A sacrament is something we do formally *on the outside* to show that God is working on the inside. We refuse to define how God is present in the Word and sacraments. However, we suffice it to say that we believe He is with us and affirm that whatever God needs to do when He is present, God will accomplish. The prophet Isaiah spoke about the Word of God:

For as the rain cometh down, and the snow from heaven,
and returneth not thither, but watereth the earth, and
maketh it bring forth and bud, that it may give seed to
the sower, and bread to the eater: So shall my word be
that goeth forth out of my mouth: it shall not return unto
me void, but it shall accomplish that which I please, and
it shall prosper in the thing whereto I sent it.

Isaiah 55:10-11 (KJV)

From The Ground Of Our Unity, We Say:

The Triune God as revealed in the Holy Scripture of the Old and New Testaments is the only source of our life and salvation; and this Scripture is the sole standard of the doctrine and faith of the Unitas Fratrum and therefore shapes our life.

The Unitas Fratrum recognizes the Word of the Cross as the center of Holy Scripture and of all preaching of the Gospel, and it sees its primary mission, and its reason for being, to consist in bearing witness to this joyful message. We ask our Lord for power never to stray from this.

The Unitas Fratrum takes part in the continual search for sound doctrine. In interpreting Scripture and in the communication of doctrine in the Church, we look to two millennia of ecumenical Christian tradition and wisdom of our Moravian forbears in the faith to guide us as we pray for fuller understanding and ever clearer proclamation of the Gospel of Jesus Christ. But just as the Holy Scripture does not contain any doctrinal system, so the Unitas Fratrum also has not developed any of its own because it knows that the mystery of Jesus Christ, which is attested to in the Bible, cannot be comprehended completely by any human mind or expressed completely in any human statement. Also it is true that through the Holy Spirit the recognition of God's will for salvation in the Bible is revealed completely and clearly.

(The Ground of the Unity, paragraph 4)

In the Scriptures, God teaches us about Himself. Therefore, each individual benefits from learning all we can about the Bible. It is the one foundation we can all begin with and return to together as we ask the Lord to show us more. In the Sacraments God reveals himself as well in the experience of Baptism and Communion. Participation in the Sacraments gives us a common experience of work only the Lord can do.

In Essentials Unity

Moravians confess that our understanding of God's revelation is still incomplete. We, therefore, refuse to argue matters of doctrine and avoid the development of statements of faith that become binding upon others. We do, however, recognize creeds which were developed by the ancient Christian church and during the Reformation. There, the main doctrines of the Christian faith find clear and simple expression. Ideally, when questions of faith arise, we begin with the person of Christ and His Word, and enter a search for His will together. While we may reach different conclusions, we covenant to remain united, not in opinion, but in Jesus. We trust that God will accomplish His will through the hearts and lives of those who seek Him. In place of drafting statements to legislate our belief, we describe the relational harmony we seek together by the motto: *In essentials, unity; In non-essentials, liberty; In all things, love.*

In the various provinces of the *Moravian Church* around the world, the following statements of faith in particular gained special importance, because in them the main doctrines of the Christian faith find clear and simple expression:

- **The Apostles' Creed**
- **The Athanasian Creed**
- **The Nicene Creed**
- **The Confession of the Unity of the Bohemian Brethren of 1535**
- **The Twenty-one Articles of the unaltered Augsburg Confession**
- **The Shorter Catechism of Martin Luther**
- **The Synod of Berne of 1532**
- **The Thirty-nine Articles of the Church of England**
- **The Theological Declaration of Barmen of 1934**
- **The Heidelberg Catechism**

The ancient *Unity of the Brethren* divided matters of faith into three categories: *essentials, ministerials (sometimes called auxiliaries)*, and ***incidentals*** *(sometimes called accidentals)*. *Essential* things pertaining to God are the will and grace of God, the Father for our salvation, the merit of Christ the Son, and the gifts of the Holy Spirit. *Essential* on the believer's part was to exhibit faith, love, and hope. *Ministerial* things are those by which the essentials are made known, conferred, and appropriated. The Scriptures, the authority of the Church and its disciplines, and the sacraments are the means by which we receive and practice the essentials. *Incidental* things refer to the time, place, and method of exercising the ministerial things.

Moravians believe that through the Scriptures, God reveals Himself and teaches us what is in His heart. In some places God's will is very clear. When the Scriptures determine something as binding, we seek to be of one heart and mind in our teaching, practice, and belief. Where the meaning of Scripture is unclear we refuse to argue about it or make the matter binding on others. There is a certain freedom to practice whatever grows a believer's relationship with God, while not hindering others.

One example of such openness to diverse interpretation is over what actually happens to the bread and the cup when believers take communion. Jesus doesn't detail the change either for the bread and cup, or the believer's life, other than to say: *"Do this in remembrance of me."* We suffice it to say that communion is *"that place where our hearts and the Savior meet."* This allows for great diversity in the expression of faith in action of non-essential matters as long as we weigh carefully how our decisions will affect others. We do not wish to cause harm or confusion to other people because of a personal determination of faith. Instead, we endeavor to put on the love of God for them that the way we live our lives will point others to Christ.

This emphasis of personal responsibility to seek understanding of the heart of God leads the Moravian Church to shy away from making position statements as a body. Instead, we trust that the witness of the church is borne out in the collection of individuals sincerely grappling with God's will on a daily basis in this world. This can lead to frustration when Moravians come together to deal with controversial issues within our culture, which arouse deeply personal sentiments. There is a certain discomfort that the church accepts for the ongoing privilege to suffer in the awkward pursuit of God's will. In theory, we have a confidence that as we come to Christ together to share what God is teaching us individually from His Word, He will work out a corporate proclamation of Jesus applicable to the various fields of witness to which we each will go. Rather than church pronouncements, the truth of God's Word is best proclaimed in the actions of our lives.

GROWTH ASSIGNMENT

Can you make a list of your beliefs you know are essential? Can you make a list of beliefs which would be areas of more of your personal preference, but not essential for all Christians? What are some specific questions you have for God about areas that are not clear?

So What Do We Believe?

One of the earliest statements of faith for Christians was the Apostles' Creed. Written in the second century A.D., this statement of faith simply expresses the key tenets of Christian belief.

I believe in God, the Father Almighty,
Creator of heaven and earth.
I believe in Jesus Christ, His only Son, our Lord.
He was conceived by the power of the Holy Spirit
and born of the Virgin Mary.
He suffered under Pontius Pilate,
was crucified, died, and was buried.
He descended to the dead.
On the third day He rose again.
He ascended into heaven and is seated at the right hand
of the Father.
He will come again to judge the living and the dead.
I believe in the Holy Spirit,
the Holy Christian* Church,
the communion of saints,

the forgiveness of sins,
the resurrection of the body,
and the life everlasting. Amen.

*Ancient text reads, "catholic," which means "universal."

We Believe In God, The Father Almighty, Creator Of Heaven And Earth

While we make no binding statements of faith for all Moravians, The *Easter Morning Liturgy* of resurrection comes closest to expressing a uniquely Moravian belief. Regarding God the Father, we find:

> *We believe in the one only God, Father, Son, and Holy Spirit, who created all things by Jesus Christ, and was in Christ, reconciling the world to himself. We believe in God, the Father of our Lord Jesus Christ, who has chosen us in Christ before the foundation of the world; who has rescued us from the power of darkness and has brought us into the kingdom of his beloved Son; who has blessed us in Christ with all spiritual blessings; who has made us worthy to share in the inheritance of the saints, having destined us for adoption as his children through Jesus Christ, according to the good pleasure of God's will, to the praise of his glorious grace.*
>
> *(Moravian Book of Worship, page 82)*

GROWTH ASSIGNMENT

What have you experienced about God as Father that you would add? Are there other images you would use to describe God as your creator and sustainer?

We Believe In Jesus Christ, His Only Son, Our Lord

The central and most significant portion of the *Apostles' Creed* is the statement about Jesus. Jesus plays the central role in our knowledge of God and in the experience of our salvation. As previously mentioned, the person of Jesus is central to the Moravian Church because the relationship with Jesus is essential to salvation and our inheritance as children of God. It is difficult to speak with clarity about the things of God, the Infinite Father, and of the unseen Spirit. But we can speak boldly about the experience of what Jesus has done for us.

The *Easter Morning Liturgy* continues:

> *We believe in the only Son of God, by whom all things in heaven and on earth were created. We believe that he became flesh and lived among us, taking the form of a servant. Since we are flesh and blood, he himself became a human being. By the overshadowing of the Holy Spirit, he was conceived of the Virgin Mary. He was born of a woman; and, being found in human form, was in every respect tempted as we are, yet without sin. For he is the Lord, the messenger of the covenant, in whom we delight. The Spirit of the Lord sent Jesus to proclaim the time of the Lord's favor. He spoke of what he knew and testified to what he had seen. To all who receive him, who believe in his name, he gives power to become children of God. We believe in Jesus Christ, the Lamb of God, who takes away the sin of the world, suffered under Pontius Pilate, was crucified, died, and was buried. He descended to the dead. On the third day he rose again. He ascended into heaven, and is seated at the right hand of the Father. He will come again in the same way as he was seen going into heaven...*
>
> *This we truly believe. This is my Lord, who redeemed me, a lost and condemned human creature, from sin, from death, and from the power of the devil; not with gold or silver, but with his holy, precious blood, and with his innocent suffering and dying. Christ has done this so that I may be his own, live in his kingdom, and serve him in eternal righteousness, innocence, and happiness, since he, being risen from the dead, lives and reigns forever and ever.*
>
> (Moravian Book of Worship, pages 83-84)

Moravians are called *christo-centric* or **Christ-centered** because of a simple insistence on the relationship with Christ as the heart of Christian belief. Long before it was popular, Moravians sought to demonstrate their point of reference for all of life with a question similar to; *"What would Jesus do?"*; *"How is your heart with the Savior?"* The aim of a life centered on Christ Jesus has the goal of becoming like Him so that wherever Moravians might go, others will know of the life transforming power and presence of the person of the Son of God.

> *For I decided to know nothing among you except Jesus Christ and him crucified.*
> 1 Corinthians 2:2 (RSV)

> *For God was pleased to have all his fullness dwell in him (Jesus), and through him to reconcile to himself all things, whether things on earth or things in heaven, by making peace through his blood, shed on the cross.*
> Colossians 1:19-20 (NIV)

GROWTH ASSIGNMENT

What is the condition of your relationship with Jesus? What has Jesus shown you or done in your life? Is there anything you would like to ask Jesus to do in your life today?

We Believe In The Holy Spirit

The third way God reveals Himself to us is as *Spirit*. It was God's Spirit that brooded over creation in the first chapter of Genesis.

> *And the earth was without form, and void; and darkness was upon the face of the deep. And the Spirit of God moved upon the face of the waters.*
> Genesis 1:2 (KJV)

It was God's Spirit that was breathed into inert clay to bring life to the first human beings.

*Then the LORD God formed man of dust from the
ground, and breathed into his nostrils the breath of life;
and man became a living being.*

Genesis 2:7 (NAS)

Jesus told his followers they needed to wait in Jerusalem
to receive the Spirit before they would be able to do the
work of the Kingdom of God.

*While staying with them, he ordered them not to leave
Jerusalem, but to wait there for the promise of the Father.
"This," he said, "is what you have heard from me . . .
But you will receive power when the Holy Spirit has
come upon you; and you will be my witnesses in
Jerusalem, in all Judea and Samaria, and to the ends of
the earth."*

Acts 1:4 & 8 (NRSV)

*When the day of Pentecost came, they were all together
in one place. Suddenly a sound like the blowing of a
violent wind came from heaven and filled the whole
house where they were sitting. They saw what seemed to
be tongues of fire that separated and came to rest on each
of them. All of them were filled with the Holy Spirit and
began to speak in other tongues as the Spirit enabled
them.*

Acts 2:1-4 (NIV)

The word *spirit* means *wind* or *breath*. The breath of God
is called the *Holy Spirit*. It is the same Holy Spirit that we
believe was breathed upon the Moravian Church in
Herrnhut in August of 1727 to revive them and re-focus
their vision to serve Christ. It is the Spirit that
supernaturally empowers and directs the Church to
accomplish the will of God. It is the Holy Spirit that unites
us in answer to Jesus' prayer that we would be one as He is
one with the Father (John 17). It is the Spirit of God that
calls each person individually and leads each one to the
recognition of sin and openness to receive redemption in
Jesus Christ. The intimate experience of God that we call

fellowship or unity (*koinonia* in Greek) with one another is really a description of the gift only the Holy Spirit can achieve.

In the *Easter Morning Liturgy* we say:

> *We believe in the Holy Spirit, who comes from the Father, and whom our Lord Jesus Christ sent, after he went away, to be with us forever; to comfort us as a mother comforts her children; to help us in our weakness and intercede for us with sighs too deep for words; to bear witness with our spirit that we are children of God and teach us to cry, "Abba, Father;" to pour God's love into our hearts and make our bodies God's holy temple; and to work in us the will of God, allotting gifts to each one individually, just as the Spirit chooses. We believe that by our own reason and strength, we cannot believe in Jesus Christ our Lord or come to him; but that the Holy Spirit calls us through the gospel, enlightens us with the gifts of grace, dedicates us to God, and preserves us in the true faith, just as the Spirit calls, gathers, enlightens, and dedicates to God the whole church on earth, which he keeps with Jesus Christ in the only true faith. In this Christian church God daily and completely forgives us and every believer all our sin.*
>
> *(Moravian Book of Worship, page 85)*

GROWTH ASSIGNMENT

What images come to your mind when you hear of the "work of the Holy Spirit?" If the Holy Spirit is the unseen force of God, much as the wind would move a sailing ship on the ocean, what needs might you have for spiritual power to blow from God through your life? Is there someone or some place or activity to which you believe God's wind might move you?

You might wish to pray this prayer that we pray each Pentecost for the Holy Spirit to come in your life:

> *Come, heavenly Dove, and alight upon us. Anoint us to bring good news to the poor, to proclaim release, recovery, and freedom to those in need. Empower us to work for God's kingdom in such a way that life becomes a Jubilee,*

for us and for all people. Lift up the lonely, the neglected, the outcast. Comfort the grieving. Restore the lost. Be the advocate of the afflicted. Teach all your people. Remind us of Jesus, and lead us into all the truth. Keep us on the edge of dynamic living, wrapped in the flames of new beginnings and filled with power for personal renewal. Form us in the likeness of Christ, that we may glorify God's name. Renew your church. Fill stagnant and empty lives with the breath of God. Overcome our apathy, and energize us with your engaging presence. Give your church new vision, new hope, and a driving desire to claim the promise of new birth. Spirit of power, work in all who confess the risen Christ to spread your message of hope, love, and salvation to every person and nation. Hasten the day when every tongue will confess that Jesus Christ is Lord!

(Moravian Book of Worship, pages 98-99)

We Believe In The Holy Christian Church

Moravians believe that by holy baptism we are made members of the Church of Christ. Jesus loves this Church and gave Himself in order to make it whole, cleansing it by water through the Word. It is Jesus' Church that He called into being to continue the proclamation of His work and of His love for all the world. We believe and confess a certain unity of the Church of Jesus Christ that was given to us by the Lord Himself. There are no labels in Jesus' Church of "Moravian" or any other delineation. Jesus died that He might gather all the scattered children of God. Those responding to Him are His living body. We believe that Jesus is our loving Lord and, as Shepherd, is leading His flock, the Church, toward such a unity. We remember well the powerfully unifying experience that is the Holy Spirit's gift when Christians confess their inability to make the perfect church and express their desperate need for the Lord. Only God can bring about His true church.

But speaking the truth in love, we are to grow up in all aspects into Him, who is the Head, even Christ, from

whom the whole body, being fitted and held together by
that which every joint supplies, according to the proper
working of each individual part, causes the growth of the
body for the building up of itself in love.
                              Ephesians 4:15-16 (NAS)

We recognize through the grace of Christ that different churches have received a variety of gifts. It is our desire that we may learn from each other and rejoice together in the richness of the love of Christ in the many-sided wisdom of God. We also confess our share of guilt over the severed and divided state of Christianity. By means of such divisions, we ourselves hinder the message and power of the gospel. We recognize the dangers of self-righteousness and of judging others without love. We also recognize the dangers of not holding fast to Scripture as the sole standard of our doctrine and faith. Since we together with all Christians are pilgrims on the way to meeting our Lord, we welcome every step that brings us nearer to the goal of unity in Him.

He Himself invites us to communion in the Lord's Supper. Through communion He leads His church toward the union that He has promised. In this true Church,

God daily and completely forgives us and every believer
all our sin.
                    (Moravian Book of Worship, page 85)

It's by means of His presence in Holy Communion that He makes our unity in Him evident and certain even today. The Church of Jesus Christ, despite all the human distinctions of male and female, the variety of skin colors, poor and rich is one in its Lord. Paul wrote to the Church in Ephesus as it struggled with how different people could be one:

Make every effort to keep the unity of the Spirit through
the bond of peace. There is one body and one Spirit - just
as you were called to one hope when you were called -
one Lord, one faith, one baptism; one God and Father of

all, who is over all and through all and in all. But to each one of us grace has been given as Christ apportioned it."

Ephesians 4:3-7 (NIV)

The *Unity of the Brethren* recognizes no distinction between those who are one in the Lord Jesus Christ. For this reason the Church believes it a higher goal to bring people into the kingdom of our Lord than to make members of the denomination. We are called to testify that God in Jesus Christ brings His people out of every race, kindred, and tongue into one body. He pardons each sinner beneath the cross and brings us together; *"But I, when I am lifted up from the earth, will draw all men to myself"* (John 12:32). Therefore, we oppose any discrimination in our midst because of race, gender, or standing, and regard it as a command of the Lord to bear public witness to this and to demonstrate in word and deed that we are brothers and sisters in Christ. We have His work to do. Jesus Christ came not to be served but to serve.

For even the Son of Man did not come to be served but to serve, and to give up his life as a ransom for many.

Mark 10:45 (NEB)

It is from Him that His church receives its mission and its power for service to which each of its members is called. We believe that the Lord has called us as His Church particularly to mission service among the peoples of the world. In this and in all other forms of service at home and abroad the Lord expects us to confess Him and witness to His love in unselfish service.

GROWTH ASSIGNMENT

Can you think of people types that are more difficult for you to love and accept? Who are some people groups that are overlooked by the Church? How could you pray for them?

We Believe In The Communion Of Saints

Through baptism, communion, and the Word of God we believe that we are given an experience of Jesus that defies definition. Through these experiences, however, we gain an intimate fellowship with those who have loved Him as Lord and Savior, not only across the world, but also across time. We have a certain oneness with the faithful who have gone before us. Rather than see ourselves called to gaze longingly at the heroes and heroines of faith, it is they who are watching and cheering us on.

These were all commended for their faith, yet none of them received what had been promised. God had planned something better for us so that only together with us would they be made perfect. Therefore, since we are surrounded by such a great cloud of witnesses, let us throw off everything that hinders and the sin that so easily entangles, and let us run with perseverance the race marked out for us. Let us fix our eyes on Jesus, the author and perfecter of our faith, who for the joy set before him endured the cross, scorning its shame, and sat down at the right hand of the throne of God.

Hebrews 11:39 -12:2 (NIV)

GROWTH ASSIGNMENT

Who are your favorite heroes or heroines of faith? Can you think of the saints who first made you aware of the love of Jesus for you? Why not give thanks for them now?

We Believe In The Forgiveness Of Sins

We have a problem with sin. God's plan is that we would be with Him forever. But sin, our separation from God, is in the way. We recognize ourselves to be a church of sinners. We are not able to live rightly and perfectly. And therefore, we require forgiveness daily and live only through the mercy of God through Christ Jesus our Lord.

Out of the depths I have cried to You, O LORD; Lord, hear my voice! Let Your ears be attentive to the voice of

my supplications. If You, LORD, should mark iniquities,
O Lord, who could stand? But there is forgiveness with
You, that You may be feared.

Psalm 130:1-4 (NKJV)

We believe that His forgiveness is complete and necessary for salvation:

This is my Lord who redeemed me, a lost and condemned
human creature from sin, from death, and from the power of
the devil, not with gold or silver, but with his holy, precious
blood, and with his innocent suffering and dying. Christ has
done this so that I may be his own, live in his kingdom and
serve him in eternal righteousness, innocence, and
happiness, since he, being risen from the dead, lives and
reigns forever and ever.

(Moravian Book of Worship, page 84)

Forgiveness of our sins comes through the work of Jesus and our relationship with Him. He treats us as though we have not sinned (even though we have). Without forgiveness we have no way past our separation from God into the eternal presence of our Lord. Our ability to receive forgiveness is directly related to our willingness to offer forgiveness to others. When Jesus taught us the Lord's Prayer He said:

And forgive us our sins, for we ourselves forgive everyone
who is indebted to us.

Luke 11:4 (RSV)

For some, accepting forgiveness and living as though our sins are no longer counted against us is difficult, because we remember our sin. When remembering his adultery, King David wrote:

For I acknowledge my transgressions: and my sin is ever
before me.

Psalm 51:3 (KJV)

Remembering repented and confessed sin can serve to humble us with the memory of how easily we can fall and bring us to daily gratitude for the love and mercy of Jesus. There may also be ongoing consequences of our sin for which we are yet responsible. It is one thing to remember repented and confessed sin. It is another to continue to hold the sin against yourself in condemnation. When we do not accept forgiveness, we are unable to grow in the life that God intends for us.

GROWTH ASSIGNMENT

Are you aware of some unforgiven sin "ever before you"? As you read this is there someone else from whom you have withheld forgiveness? What is God saying to you as you consider this advice from the Apostle John? Are there any specific sins about which you need to pray?

> *If we claim to be without sin, we deceive ourselves and the truth is not in us. If we confess our sins, he is faithful and just and will forgive us our sins and purify us from all unrighteousness. If we claim we have not sinned, we make him out to be a liar and his word has no place in our lives. My dear children, I write this to you so that you will not sin. But if anybody does sin, we have one who speaks to the Father in our defense - Jesus Christ, the Righteous One. He is the atoning sacrifice for our sins, and not only for ours, but also for the sins of the whole world.*
>
> *1 John 1:8-2:2 (NIV)*

We Believe In The Resurrection Of The Body And Life Everlasting

The earliest statement of Christian faith comes from the first Easter morning when those who went to the tomb saw with their own eyes that Jesus had been raised to life: *"The Lord is risen! The Lord is risen, indeed!" (Moravian Book of Worship, pages 82 & 90).* They shout the gospel's theme: not only was Jesus raised bodily to life, victorious over sin, but also over every power that might hold us apart from God. We believe that because of His resurrection and our life in

Him that even though we die, we will be raised from the dead ourselves.

> *But in fact Christ has been raised from the dead, the first fruits of those who have died. For since death came through a human being, the resurrection of the dead has also come through a human being; for as all die in Adam, so all will be made alive in Christ.*
> *1 Corinthians 15:20-22 (NRSV)*

Thus, when we die, our bodies rest in hope that the God of peace who brought back from the dead our Lord Jesus Christ, that Great Shepherd of the sheep, by the blood of the eternal covenant will also give life to our mortal bodies, if the Spirit of God has dwelt in us. Death is not to be feared, because we know that Jesus has defeated death's power over us.

> *When the perishable has been clothed with the imperishable, and the mortal with immortality, then the saying that is written will come true: "Death has been swallowed up in victory." Where, O death, is your victory? Where, O death is your sting? The sting of death is sin, and the power of sin is the law. But thanks be to God! He gives us the victory through our Lord Jesus Christ.*
> *1 Corinthians 15:54-57 (NIV)*

Moravians believe they will be raised with Jesus in eternity, but we do not spend time in great debate about the details about that resurrection. Paul says that our bodies will be changed (Philippians 3:21). We do not know exactly how, but are confident that when we die, we go to sleep in the arms of Jesus to await the resurrection from the dead - unless He comes before we die.

Eternity begins the moment we invite Christ into our hearts as Lord and Savior. Salvation begins in us a work of Jesus that never ends. In fact, there is still much work to be done in this world. There are still thousands of people groups in the world without the message of salvation in

Jesus. He commissioned the Church to proclaim the love-work of God to the ends of the earth until He returns. Each time we share communion we repeat the promise:

> Whenever you eat this bread and drink this cup, you proclaim the Lord's death, **Until He comes!"**
> *(Moravian Book of Worship, Services for Holy Communion, pages: various)*

Jesus has gone to prepare a place for those who love Him to be with Him forever. And Jesus is coming back to claim the Church as His Bride.

> There are many dwelling places in my Father's house; if it were not so I should have told you; for I am going there on purpose to prepare a place for you. And if I go and prepare a place for you, I shall come again and receive you to myself, so that where I am you may be also.
> *John 14:2-3 (NEB)*

There is much in the scriptures that speaks of things to come. Many Old Testament prophecies are yet to be fulfilled. In the New Testament, the teachings of Jesus, the writings of Paul and Peter, and John's Revelation all point forward to the expectation of things to come. We do not spend much time debating dates and times. We do, however, expect that He will come to usher in the final scene of this world. He comes first for His Church, then, to bring judgment. In the meantime, we have much work to do. This hymn summarizes our attitude of what is yet to come:

> Lord, for thy coming us prepare;
> may we, to meet thee without fear,
> at all times ready be;
> in faith and love preserve us sound;
> O let us day and night be found
> waiting with joy to welcome thee.
> *(Moravian Book of Worship, page 8)*

When Jesus takes us to be with Him forever, we will surround the throne of God and shout forever, with all the great multitude from every nation, tribe, people, and language:

> *"Salvation to our God who sits on the throne, and to the Lamb."*
>
> Revelation 7:10 (NAS)

GROWTH ASSIGNMENT

If Jesus were to come today, would you be ready for Him? Think of all the Lord has done for you before you knew Him. Can you recognize all that God is doing in you right now? Imagine that the best is yet to come. Most amazing of all is that you can know the same love of God today that will be with you forever simply by asking.

> *Neither height nor depth, nor anything else in all creation, will be able to separate us from the love of God that is in Christ Jesus our Lord.*
>
> Romans 8:39 (NIV)

Chapter Six

WORSHIP

WHEN WE CONSIDER WORSHIP in the Church, it is tempting to think in terms of what we *"get out"* of any given experience. It is natural to assess the things people do in worship services in terms of what worship does for us. But the English word *"worship"* actually means *"to give worth or value to."* The Scriptures agree. In the Bible we see a picture of worship as whatever time and process will recognize and celebrate the value or worth of God. People offer worship "service" to and for the Lord.

> *Come to him, a living stone, though rejected by mortals yet chosen and precious in God's sight, and like living stones, let yourselves be built into a spiritual house, to be a holy priesthood, to offer spiritual sacrifices acceptable to God through Jesus Christ.*
>
> *1 Peter 2:4-5 (NRSV)*

Serving God is not the passive activity of sitting around until God does something. Rather, *waiting upon the Lord* is much like the *"waiting"* that you expect to receive when you go to your favorite restaurant. You rate the *"service"* of those who wait upon you by how attentive those providing service are to the wishes and needs of those paying the cost. When the focus is on Jesus it is actually our worship service which is measured by God.

Have you ever imagined yourself as waiting upon the Lord? How do you think God might rate your service?

Who Does Worship, Anyway?

God is the center of worship. It is God's idea that we worship Him. He takes pleasure from the love and undivided attention of His children.

> *The LORD taketh pleasure in them that fear Him, in those that hope in His mercy.*
>
> *Psalm 147:11 (KJV)*

Our call and reason for being in worship is because God made us to know Him intimately and glorify Him. This happens when we serve the Lord. Since our goal is to experience Christ, corporate worship is whatever we must do together to prepare ourselves to meet Christ, to encounter or hear the Lord, and to respond to what we have learned from God. Paul wrote about such service when he wrote to the Christians in Rome:

> *Therefore, I urge you, brothers, in view of God's mercy, to offer your bodies as living sacrifices, holy and pleasing to God - this is your spiritual act of worship. Do not conform any longer to the pattern of this world, but be transformed by the renewing of your mind, then you will be able to test and approve what God's will is - his good, pleasing and perfect will.*
>
> *Romans 12:1-2 (NIV)*

Worship, in a sense, is the act of placing our bodies in the offering plate. We determine that the way our bodies are used will not try to *"fit in with"* the rest of the world, but be willing to be *transformed* to learn to think God's thoughts and put them into action. Living according to God's way is therefore the most reasonable or spiritual worship activity we can do. The primary place of worship is not the church building, but our bodies.

> *Do you not know that your body is a temple of the Holy Spirit within you, which you have from God? You are not your own; you were bought with a price. So glorify God in your body.*
>
> 1 Corinthians 6:19-20 (RSV)

The ultimate test of worship is whether God is worshiped. Every worship experience is a rehearsal for eternity, not a test whether we have more people in worship than one year ago, or than a church down the block. We have the opportunity to practice life in the immediate presence of God each time we meet in His name. We help one another most when we live in expectation of the nearness of God and the perfect experience of worship yet to come. We help non-believers most when our *"having been with the Lord"* becomes evident when we are with them.

When we come together for corporate worship we are the Body of Christ. We are built up in the joyful knowledge that God has been at work through each of us while we were apart; we are unified in our common need for Jesus; and we are woven together as we experience Him among us. But worship service doesn't end when the corporate gathering is finished. Our Body life and service continues 24 hours a day by those who have committed to put into action the change wrought by the experience of God.

GROWTH ASSIGNMENT

What are some changes God has made in your life through worship? Would anything be different about the way you live your life if your worship service lasted 24 hours a day?

Worship Centers On Jesus As The Chief Object

What brought us together, what joined our hearts?
The pardon which Jesus, our High Priest, imparts;
'Tis this which cements the disciples of Christ,
who are into one by the Spirit baptized.

Is this our high calling, harmonious to dwell,
and thus in sweet concert Christ's praises to tell,
in peace and blessed union our moments to spend
and live in communion with Jesus our Friend?

O yes, having found in the Lord our delight,
he is our chief object by day and by night;
this knits us together; no longer we roam;
we all have one Father, and heav'n is our home.

(Moravian Book of Worship, Hymn 675)

The principal characteristic of Moravian worship is that it is centered on Jesus. The primary object of each worship experience is to connect the heart of the believer with the Savior. Moravian worship space is generally simple and relatively unadorned. The focal point in the room is the place where Jesus is most recognized as being present: in the Word and Sacraments; by His promise to be among us whenever we gather in His name; and in the temple of each believer's heart. This usually means the communion table and preaching lectern are placed so as to draw all attention to the Lord.

Since much of Moravian worship tradition developed during times of persecution, a great variety of spaces were used to experience God. As a result, instead of a formal sanctuary or cathedral, wherever the children of God make Jesus the center of attention becomes an acceptable place of worship. Understandably, those places where we regularly enjoy deep and moving experiences of God become for us holy or special places. But it is not the place that becomes so special and holy to us, but what God does among the people gathered in His name. Even the order of the service follows a form shaped by the central message of the Word and sacraments. The Scriptures and what God has to say are the hub around which worship is developed.

GROWTH ASSIGNMENT

Are there any places in your life which seem to be more special or holy than others? What experiences of God have you had in those places for which you can give thanks? Are there any other things you notice which compete with Jesus as center of the church's attention in worship?

Worship Involves Everyone

The earliest Moravian reformers put Scripture and worship in the language of the people to engage all believers in a relationship with God. *"How are people to hear the Lord if they cannot understand?"* When worshipers feel like outsiders they are inhibited from connecting to God. It is difficult to be continually open to the language and culture of the people. Language and culture are changing constantly. On the other hand, it is human nature to become set in our ways as we gravitate toward the comfortable. Our spiritual heritage challenges us to reach toward the ideal of "daily reform," that we might communicate the un-changing message of God to an ever-changing world. This is not only a matter of translating the Gospel across language barriers, but also across the barriers between those who have been in church their whole lives and those who have not. The language and style of worship at its best ought to reflect the language of those the Church hopes to reach for God. One exciting fruit from this commitment to the language of the people is the indigenous expressions of faith throughout the provinces of the Unity of the Brethren around the world. Many native cultures were preserved by missionaries who translated Scripture and worship into local tongues in the belief that every tongue deserved to praise and proclaim the Savior.

Moravian worship is participatory. Worship is not done for us by the pastor or the choir, it is done by us. Characteristic of early reform was that all believers were encouraged to participate in worship. Ordained Moravian clergy are not separated from the people into a special spiritual category. In fact, our pastors are viewed as fellow members except when they function in administering the sacraments. They are *"ordained"* or set apart to act on behalf of Christ for the Church. Otherwise pastors are to use their own gifts in leadership to equip the members of the body to offer their gifts to God.

> *It was he who gave some to be apostles, some to be prophets, some to be evangelists, and some to be pastors and teachers, to prepare God's people for works of service, so that the body of Christ may be built up until we all reach unity in the faith and in the knowledge of the Son of God and become mature, attaining to the whole measure of the fullness of Christ.*
>
> Ephesians 4:11-13 (NIV)

Gifts include service as musicians, ushers, nursery caretakers, *dieners (German, for servers)*, intercessors, preachers, readers, healers, generous givers, etc. Many cherished traditions arose out of the search to provide means for worshipers to participate more fully in the worship event. The various gifts that God has given to each believer are valued personal offerings to be made to God. The whole church is built up and grows in its ability to experience and magnify the Lord as the diverse gifts and testimonies of its people are given opportunity to be shared.

GROWTH ASSIGNMENT

What are some of the aspects of worship that are difficult for you to understand or relate to? Are you aware of any personal gifts God has given you to use in worship?

A Church Of Musicians

One of the easiest ways to include people in participation to worship God is through singing, playing, and composing music. There is something about song that is able to express deep things of the heart which simple words alone cannot. Moravian worship is traditionally rich with music. We recognize the value of hymns which state the faith of the Church through the ages and at the same time rejoice in new expressions of praise inspired from among the living. New hymn writing has been especially prolific during periods of great spiritual growth throughout the Church's history. During some years of the 1700's, members wrote new hymns for each worship service. Some of these hymns had value for only one occasion. Others have continued in use through the years. All of them, however, were expressions of people thoroughly involved in offering gifts of worship to their Lord and Savior.

Publishing the first Protestant hymnal in 1501, the Unity of the Brethren has continued to develop hymnals to remain current and inclusive of the dynamically changing worship material. Whereas 15th century innovations in worship music included writing the words to hymns in Czech on the church walls, in the 18th century creative use of instrumentation was encouraged to accompany worship services. Today, it may mean being open to styles of music more representative of the culture of America in the 21st century.

Praise the Lord. Praise God in His sanctuary;
Praise Him in His mighty firmament!
Praise Him for His mighty acts;
Praise Him according to His excellent greatness!
Praise Him with the sound of the trumpet;
Praise Him with the lute and harp!
Praise Him with the timbrel and dance;
Praise Him with stringed instruments and flutes!
Praise Him with loud cymbals;
Praise Him with clashing cymbals!
Let everything that has breath praise the Lord.
Praise the Lord!
Psalm 150 (NKJV)

Members are often encouraged to learn to play musical

instruments as well that all might have some role in glorifying God. This was particularly useful in early Colonial America where Moravian colonists brought portable worship ensembles of strings, wood-winds, and brass. Ensembles could be found playing hymns in the fields during breaks from farm work. Some of the finest examples of early Colonial American music come from Moravian musicians giving expression to their faith.

The last century has seen a dramatic increase in the variety of instrumentation. Our heritage of *participation for everyone* would suggest that there is a place in worship for any gift that will glorify God. As styles of music change, the church that struggled to put worship into the language of 15th century people has the ongoing challenge for worship to be the indigenous expression of worshipers in the 21st. Many worship attitudes of the Church today were formed around needs and gifts of other eras of church experience. The first-century church had no organ, yet they were encouraged to speak to one another with *"psalms, hymns, and spiritual songs"* (Ephesians 5:19). The song leader for Psalm 150 seems to capture best the heart of Moravian worship music. We see through the psalmist a worship experience that looks to bring every possible instrument and voice available to honor and adore God: *Let everything that has breath praise the Lord!* (Psalm 150:6). In our picture of eternity all the saints of Jesus will worship Him who sits on the throne to His honor and praise:

Sing hallelujah, praise the Lord!
Sing with a cheerful voice;
exalt our God with one accord,
and in his name rejoice!
Ne'er cease to sing, O ransomed host,
praise Father, Son, and Holy Ghost,
until in realms of endless light
your praises shall unite.

There we to all eternity
shall join the angelic lays
and sing in perfect harmony

to God our Savior's praise;
he has redeemed us by his blood,
and made us kings and priests to God;
for us, for us, the Lamb was slain!
Praise ye the Lord! Amen.
(Moravian Book of Worship, Hymn 543)

GROWTH ASSIGNMENT

What music helps you most to connect with God? What is your favorite song of faith? If you were to write your own song of praise, what would be your theme?

Form With Freedom

The principle guide to our worship life is the person of Jesus as revealed in His Word and the sacraments. We trust that the Holy Spirit will direct us in the development and conducting of any worship experience. Therefore, there is great freedom under God's guidance to use any given service that will lead us into His presence. Unrestrained expression, however, of the great diversity of both gifts and personal preferences represented in any gathering of believers can lead to confusion. The earliest Christians struggled with how God allows both for vibrant freedom with the ordered constraint of love for others.

> *To sum it up, my friends: when you meet for worship, each of you contributes a hymn, some instruction, a revelation, an ecstatic utterance, or the interpretation of such an utterance. All of these must aim at one thing: to build up the church . . . for the God who inspires them is not a God of disorder but of peace.*
>
> *1 Corinthians 14:26-33 (NEB)*

Holy Spirit guided form gives focus to inspired expression to God. Our form follows the function of what worship leaders believe will best help us experience and respond to the Lord. Some form is intentional and spoken, while other form is understood and unspoken. Moravians are considered semi-liturgical, because while we trust the

115

Word and the Spirit to develop each service, we draw upon certain tools of church order to help us approach God in worship. One of those tools is the **Moravian Book of Worship.** A quote by Nicholas Ludwig von Zinzendorf is included in the front of the hymnal. It summarizes our attitude about the *Book of Worship.*

> *"The hymnal is a kind of response to the Bible, an echo and an extension thereof. In the Bible one perceives how the Lord communicates with people; and in the hymnal, how people communicate with the Lord."*
> *(Moravian Book of Worship, page iii)*

The first part of the *Moravian Book of Worship* contains a collection of services, or liturgies, designed to lead us into the presence of God. Some of the liturgies are ancient expressions of worship of the Christian church, others are thematic. Ideally, liturgies are interactive arrangements of Scriptures, mingled with prayers and hymn verses around a common theme. They originally arose out of a desire to help people participate in worship. Some of these formal prayers represent common forms of worship which bind Moravians together throughout the world. These arrangements must never become a dead letter or degenerate into dry, cold form. It is rather, a valued principle of our church that there is liberty to introduce changes and improvements in the mode of worship according to the direction of the Holy Spirit.

The essence and soul of our worship meetings are not to be found in the form, but rather, in the religion of the heart, which is expressed in the form. Also included in the present *Moravian Book of Worship* is a collection of Psalms with optional music for chanting. Some traditions of Moravian worship find chanting particularly helpful.

The largest portion of the hymnal is the collection of hymns. No hymnal is adequate to include all expressions of worship for the whole of the Church. So, throughout history Moravians have developed new hymnals frequently. Churches are not limited to either the liturgies or the hymns in hymnals. They do, however, represent a snapshot of representative expressions of Moravian worship in a given time and culture. It is recognized that forms of worship are not ends in themselves, but means to an end, namely, the adoration of God in Jesus Christ and renewed dedication to His service.

GROWTH ASSIGNMENT

What parts of worship do you find particularly meaningful? Are there any forms of worship which you find confusing or which hinder your experience of God in worship?

The Church Year

To help ensure that the Church covers the key themes of Scripture and to allow for unity of focus throughout the world we also observe the *Church Year*. Suggested scripture passages arranged to coincide with the Church Year are called **The Lectionary.** Moravians are not bound by the Lectionary, but when followed, it serves as a tool for worship planning. It generally includes a passage from the Psalms, an Old Testament reading, a Gospel lesson, and a selection from a New Testament letter.

The *Church Year* is designed to have the church fall in step with the life and ministry of Jesus.

Advent, a Latin word which means *"coming,"* includes the four Sundays before Christmas. During *Advent* we consider the prophecies preparing the world for the coming of the Messiah. It is a reminder to proclaim His first coming to the world and to prepare for His coming again.

Christmas celebrates the incarnation of Jesus - God's Word became flesh and dwelt among us.

Epiphany means *"the shining"* or *"the showing forth."* It starts January 6 in the Western Church and continues until the beginning of *Lent.* It is during this season that the church focuses on the ministry and teachings of Jesus which demonstrate His authority and purpose as God's Son.

Lent from the Old English word for *"spring"* is the season of 40 days, not including Sundays, prior to *Easter.* Lent seeks to appreciate the sacrificial work of Jesus for our salvation. This season of spiritual preparation culminates in *"Passion Week."* Each day of this holy week before *Easter,* Moravians gather to worship, pray, and read the Gospel accounts of Jesus' teachings, suffering, and death. We consider how the death of Jesus for our sins frees us to live to serve Him.

Easter is the oldest church celebration. Christians began observing *Easter* on Sunday in honor of Jesus' resurrection. The *Easter Season* includes the 50 days after Easter in celebration of God's power over sin and death in raising Jesus to new life.

Pentecost was originally a Hebrew harvest festival, 50 days after the *Passover.* Because of the outpouring of the Holy Spirit on the church in Jerusalem (Acts 2), it has taken on new significance for Christians. The *Season of Pentecost* covers half of the church year and considers each Christian's responsibility to proclaim and bring Christ to the world. *Pentecost* remembers that Jesus promised His followers:

> *Truly, truly, I say to you, he who believes in me, the works that I do shall he do also; and greater works than these shall he do; because I go to the Father.*
> *John 14:12 (NAS)*

Pentecost ends when *Advent* begins the cycle once again.

GROWTH ASSIGNMENT

What is your favorite Season of the Church Year? Do you know what it is that makes it so special?

Unique Services Of Worship

Holy Communion

Moravians celebrate Holy Communion because Jesus instructed us to do so. The meal is sometimes called *The Lord's Supper* or *The Eucharist (Thanksgiving Meal)*. In his first letter to the Corinthians the Apostle Paul records the earliest written account of the command of Jesus concerning the Lord's supper:

> *For I received from the Lord what I also passed on to you: the Lord Jesus, on the night he was betrayed, took bread, and when he had given thanks, he broke it and said, "This is my body, which is for you; do this in remembrance of me." In the same way, after supper he took a cup, saying, "This cup is the new covenant in my blood; do this, whenever you drink it, in remembrance of me. "For whenever you eat this bread and drink this cup, you proclaim the Lord's death until he comes.*
> *1 Corinthians 11:23-26 (NIV)*

Holy Communion is a sacrament. As we **eat bread and drink the cup** on the outside, God is doing the true heart work on the inside. We believe that Jesus is present in communion. However, beyond the words of Scripture we refuse to define what happens in communion. There is a sense that whatever the Lord needs to do with a believer will take place as we partake and remember. Moravians in the 18th century were content to say: *"it is that place where the heart and the Savior meet."*

We practice open communion, which means that all baptized believers in Jesus are invited to share in God's redeeming work. Those who normally take communion in some other Christian body, are considered part of Christ's family and encouraged to participate with us. Moravian churches do not tend to offer communion every Sunday. Most communion services are linked to significant events in the church year or the life of the congregation. Believers, however, can request communion whenever deemed helpful to grow in faith.

Prior to taking communion it is important to prepare our hearts through prayer, inner examination, and humble confession. At certain times in history, and even today in certain parts of the world, those wishing to participate in communion were asked to *"speak"* to the pastor or elders to ensure the readiness, not only of each believer's heart, but of the body of faith, as well.

> *Therefore, whoever eats the bread or drinks the cup of the Lord in an unworthy manner will be guilty of sinning against the body and blood of the Lord. A man ought to examine himself before he eats of the bread and drinks of the cup. For anyone who eats and drinks without recognizing the body of the Lord eats and drinks judgment on himself.*
>
> 1 Corinthians 11:27-29 (NIV)

The form of Moravian communion celebration has varied over the years. There is no required form beyond the words of Scripture to *consecrate*, or *set aside*, the elements for God's purposes. Generally, however, certain practices are characteristic of Moravians throughout the world.

- As we begin the communion service, we take time to share the **right hand of fellowship**, shaking hands with our neighbors. We do this to signify our oneness in Christ and the desire to be at peace with one another. We all are sinners in need of His grace, mercy, and peace. At the end of communion we share the *right hand of fellowship* once again to indicate our renewed dedication and unity of purpose in the service of Christ. This gives us a common message as we go forth changed by Him.

- There is **no altar** in the simple setting of communion. It is so significant to us that Jesus' death paid the price for our sins, *once and for all*, that further sacrifice for sin is unnecessary. Therefore, instead of believers coming to the *altar*, we emphasize that Jesus brought salvation to us while we were yet sinners. The communion table is sometimes centered on the level of the congregation.

- Usually, *the congregation sings* around a theme during the serving of communion. The congregation is generally served where seated as an opportunity for each member to personally receive a gift from Jesus. We wait, however, until all have been served to eat and/or drink it together as a body.

- Pastors and other designated servers typically wear a simple white robe, called a *surplice*. Rather than a mark of distinction, the *surplice* is to remove the personality of the server so the receiver might focus on Christ.

- *Participants stand to receive* the elements, indicating both their readiness to receive the gift of Christ and show that the bread and cup are not being worshiped, but the Lord who gives them.

Lovefeast

The earliest Christians gathered each Sunday to celebrate the resurrection of Jesus. As an outgrowth of their worship experience, they shared a meal representative of the intimacy they were experiencing with Christ. These meals were known as *feasts of agape*, Greek for *love feasts.* Over the years, the Church meals lost the character of God's love, and the practice was discontinued. Amidst the outpouring of the Holy Spirit on August 13, 1727, in Herrnhut, God became powerfully present. Therefore, a simple meal was provided so that worshipers could continue sharing together. In later reflection they remarked how similar it seemed to the early church experience of the *Lovefeast.*

The meal is not a sacrament. It is a simple celebration of how powerfully the love of God has changed us all. In the United States a bun and drink of coffee or juice are typically served. In other parts of the world there is great variety in food and drink. The theme, or message, of the service is carried in the words of songs and Scripture. Food is served by members of the congregation designated as *"dieners,"* which is German for *"servers." Dieners* are known in some areas as *"sacristans." * For some Moravians, *sacristans* are those who prepare the elements necessary to celebrate the sacraments. Moravians can celebrate a Lovefeast whenever there is a particularly strong sense of the love of God at work among us.

Christmas Eve Candle Service

To help visualize the coming of Jesus with the children of the church, a pastor in Marienborn, Germany, developed a Christmas object lesson. Taking a candle, he demonstrated how Christ comes as the light of the world. As we receive Jesus into our hearts He sets our hearts on fire with love for Him and sends us out as light to the nations. Some use a red frill as further reminder that even in the birth of Jesus, His coming was to pay for our sin in His blood for our salvation.

This simple service is often combined with the *Lovefeast* as we seek to make a tangible expression of God's love in sending Jesus. This service has become one of the most beloved traditions in the Moravian Church. The rich music combined with the light of many candles filling the darkness is a very physical reminder of the intimate love of God we all so desperately need as Jesus brings light to the world.

Watchnight Service

New Year's Eve is a wonderful time to count the blessings God has bestowed on the past year, and to seek God's guidance for the future. There is such a natural opportunity to renew commitments to Christ that we want to bring in the New Year in worship. At times a "memorabilia" is prepared to reflect on God's hand at work in the Church over the past year. Scripture texts are sometimes offered as *"watchwords"* for the year to come. Not only has God been so good in the past, but we declare the good news that God will be faithful in all that is to come.

Holy Week Services

Holy Week or *Passion Week* is the week between *Palm Sunday and Easter.* Moravians gather daily to read a chronological arrangement of the Gospels' account of the events leading up to Jesus' death. The readings are mingled with song and prayer to impress upon us the *"passion"* our Lord demonstrated in showing us the greatest love when He laid down His life for His friends. The week begins with the **Palm Sunday** celebration of Jesus' entry into Jerusalem on a carpet of cloaks and palm branches to songs of *"Hosanna!"* On **Maundy Thursday** (Latin for *mandate or command*), we share the Lord's Supper in obedience to His command to *"do this in remembrance of me."* We pause in amazement on **Good Friday** beneath the cross of Jesus. It can be a time of great contrition for what our sins did to the Son of God. But more significantly, it is a statement of our gratitude for what Jesus did there to our sins!

> *O sacred head, now wounded,*
> *with grief and shame weighed down,*
> *now scornfully surrounded*
> *with thorns your only crown.*
> *O sacred head, what glory*
> *and blessing you have known!*
> *Yet, though despised and gory,*
> *I claim you as my own.*
>
> *My Lord, what you did suffer*
> *was all for sinners' gain;*
> *mine, mine was the transgression,*
> *but yours the deadly pain.*
> *So here I kneel, my Savior,*
> *for I deserve your place;*
> *look on me with your favor*
> *and save me by your grace.*

*What language shall I borrow to
thank you, dearest friend,
For this, your dying sorrow,
your mercy without end?
Lord, make me yours forever,
a loyal servant true,
and let me never, never
outlive my love for you.*
(Moravian Book of Worship, Hymn 345)

Easter Sunrise Service

The earliest Christian holiday is *Easter*. From the very earliest times after the resurrection of Jesus those who loved Him gathered to remember that the Lord who was crucified is alive! Each Sunday, in reality, is an *Easter* celebration. On *Easter Sunday* morning music and singing throughout the night often announce the coming celebration. Moravians gather in the dark, near a cemetery, if possible, to announce, *"The Lord is risen! The Lord is risen indeed!"* It is our declaration of faith that light has come into the darkness; that Jesus has overcome death, and that we who believe in Him are saved to live with Him forever. The "Easter Morning" Liturgy gives triumphant expression to the heart of our faith and proclaims the central theme of God's undying love for all.

GROWTH ASSIGNMENT

What is your favorite time of the Church year? What is God doing in you that might make such worship so meaningful? If you could ask any question about worship what would it be? Who might be able to provide the answer?

Chapter Seven

The Organization Of The Organism

IT IS THE OBJECT OF EACH CONGREGATION to be a true church of Jesus Christ and further the interest of the kingdom of God according to the teaching of His Holy Word, and according to the doctrines and practices of the Moravian Church. Such congregations don't come into being without the call and order of God's design for it. If any church is to live up to such a purpose, it must learn to work together according to the Lord's organizational structure - like a body.

> *And his gifts were that some should be apostles, some prophets, some evangelists, some pastors and teachers, to equip the saints for the work of ministry, for building up the body of Christ, until we all attain to the unity of the faith and of the knowledge of the Son of God, to mature manhood, to the measure of the stature of the fullness of Christ.*
>
> *Ephesians 4:11-13 (RSV)*

The most important part of the Body of Christ is Jesus. The most important opinion in the Church is that of Jesus. As the mission and church renewal work spread from

Herrnhut in the 1740's, church leaders quickly discovered that no human being was able to effectively be Head over the Church. Only Christ Jesus can hold each diverse part together to function for the common good. Therefore, we see it as the duty of each part of the body to live daily in an effort to discern and carry out the will of our Lord and Savior.

The Lord already knows what His will is and how He intends for believers to carry it out. In God's wisdom, the Church was organized, not around the model of a corporation, but as a living organism. God administers the working and decision making of the Church through the help of the Holy Spirit as our guide.

> *For just as we have many members in one body and all the members do not have the same function, so we, who are many, are one body in Christ, and individually members one of another. And since we have gifts that differ according to the grace given to us, let each exercise them accordingly: if prophecy, according to the proportion of his faith; if service, in his serving; or he who teaches, in his teaching; or he who exhorts, in his exhortation; he who gives, with liberality; he who leads, with diligence; he who shows mercy, with cheerfulness.*
> *Romans 12:4-8 (NAS)*

Church Council

The primary decision-making body in the local church is the **Church Council.** The *Church Council* is composed of all *communicant* members (those who have publicly professed their faith in Jesus as Lord and Savior and formally joined the congregation) of the congregation who are in good standing. It is this body's duty to discern the will of God in the election of leadership who will direct church matters between gatherings of the *Church Council* and to decide any major matters affecting the congregation. The whole Church Council meets at least once a year and any additional times as necessary.

Moravians in North America practice what is known as a "Conferencial" style of government. At its heart is the belief that each individual member is fervently and daily seeking the will of God. When we meet together to "confer" we are ideally sharing, not human opinion, but each person's best sense of the will of God. We believe that this process of discernment together will bring us all closer to what is in God's heart than any one of us alone.

Congregation Boards

Most congregations divide leadership responsibilities into two executive boards: **the Board of Elders and the Board of Trustees.** *Elders* are principally charged with the spiritual welfare of the congregation while *Trustees* are charged with the temporal concerns of the church. This is not to imply that the work of *Elders* is in any way impractical, or that the work of *Trustees* is not a spiritual ministry. In fact, church leaders are expected to exhibit a spiritual maturity before being considered ready to serve. *Elders and Trustees* are elected to limited terms of service by the congregation from among those members deemed to exhibit both the gifts and spiritual maturity to lead the church.

> *Deacons, likewise must be serious, not double-tongued, not indulging in much wine, not greedy for money; they must hold fast to the mystery of the faith with a clear conscience. And let them first be tested; then, if they prove themselves blameless, let them serve as deacons.*
> *1 Timothy 3:8-10 (NRSV)*

The Board of Elders

The Board of Elders consists of a set number of members of the congregation and the pastor who is the chairperson. A vice-chair and secretary are elected from the board members. All ministers serving under the call to a congregation are regular voting members of the Board.

The duties of the Board of Elders are to give spiritual care and oversight to the congregation. They oversee the Christian education of the members of the congregation and their instruction in the doctrine, history, principles and usages of the Moravian Church. They may plan, schedule, and publicize the various services of the church and determine the purposes for which the church building may be used. They may assist the Pastor(s) in the administration of church music and to appoint persons to assist in worship, such as organist, choir director, and ushers. They decide on matters pertaining to the admission and dismissal of members. They are involved in the appointment of non-salaried personnel such as Chief Usher, Head Denier, etc. They may determine when, how, and what appeals shall be taken for causes outside of the local congregation when not already provided for by synodal enactment.

The Board of Trustees

The Board of Trustees consists of a set number of members of the congregation and officers are elected from the membership.

The trustees are especially charged with the oversight of the temporal affairs of the congregation. They shall strive to assure the prompt payment of all salaries, bills, and all provincial and other obligations. They may plan the annual budget in consultation with the Board of Elders. They have charge of maintenance of all church property.

Each board of the congregation generally appoints committees or ministry teams to carry out specific programs. Both Boards meet together periodically, forming the Joint Board, to improve communication, and handle matters beyond either Board's duties, such as working with the Provincial Elders in the calling of a pastor. Members with questions and concerns are encouraged and expected to speak candidly with their Elders or Trustees respectively.

Pastors

Pastors are members of the local congregation, but **ordained** *(set aside to perform the sacraments)* to serve the whole denomination. *Ordination* is a matter of function, not status. Those sensing a call to pastoral ministry are encouraged to speak with their pastor and church leaders to begin a process of examination, which assesses their suitability for ministry. Approved candidates in North America are generally expected to have an undergraduate degree and then complete three years of seminary training. Graduation from seminary does not necessarily imply that a person will become a pastor. Candidates are not ordained until they receive a call to specific service.

There are three orders of ordained ministry in the Moravian Church: **Deacon, Presbyter, and Bishop.** Those who are ordained are authorized to administer the sacraments in the Moravian Church. Non-ordained persons can be licensed as "Ministers" in the Northern Province or as "Acolytes" in the Southern Province to assist in serving the sacraments under special circumstances. Pastors begin ordination as *Deacons* or *servants* of the Church. This is a period of ministry under observation and counsel by a more experienced Presbyter. After a period of time, normally three to five years, a *Deacon* may be **consecrated** or *dedicated* to God as a *Presbyter*. A *Presbyter* is a mature pastor. Consecration indicates the Church's spiritual affirmation of the individual's fruitful witness in ministry and approval of service rendered. *Bishops* have spiritual responsibility for the health of the denomination, serve as intercessors for the church, and are pastors of pastors. There is no administrative function necessarily tied to the role of *Bishop*. *Bishops* are elected by Synods from among eligible *Presbyters*.

The Call Process

Of central importance in any pastoral change is the will of God. When a vacancy occurs in a local congregation, denomination leaders meet with the *Joint Board* of that congregation to determine their needs for leadership. A prayerful and confidential search is begun to determine pastors with gifts suitable for the specific congregation's needs. When both the denomination leaders and the *Joint Board* have agreed on a particular pastor, *a call* is issued from the denomination. It is then the pastor's responsibility to discern whether God is saying "yes" or "no." Pastors are not moved on a regular basis. Ideally, pastors stay until their work in a particular setting is finished. Pastors do not interview or apply to a particular church prior to receiving a call. Congregations do not recruit or advertise for pastors to come to them. At its heart, this *call process* seeks God's will in matching pastors with churches.

The Province

Moravians understand themselves as a truly "worldwide" church, not bound by race, language, culture, or geography. Africa, Latin America, and Asia are outpacing North America and Europe as the numerical centers of world Christianity. Likewise, the vast majority of Moravians live in those rapidly expanding parts of the Church. Congregations in common geographic areas are affiliated under a regional church government called a *Province*. Each *province* orders its own affairs independently, but is subject to the general principles that set the standard of the whole *Unity of the Brethren* in doctrine, practice, and belief. This allows each area of the Moravian Church to retain an indigenous expression of faith while maintaining an essential Unity in world witness. Provinces of the Unity of the Brethren are as follows in the order of their establishment:

✝ the Czech Province (1457, renewed 1862)

✝ the European Continental Province (Sweden, Denmark, Estonia, Germany, the Netherlands, and Switzerland) (1722)

✝ the Eastern West Indies Province (the U.S. Virgin Islands, Antigua, St. Kitts, Barbados, Tobago, and Trinidad) (1732)

✝ the Suriname Province (1735)

✝ the South Africa Province (1737, renewed 1792)

✝ the Northern Province of the Moravian Church in what today is the United States and Canada (New York, New Jersey, Pennsylvania, Maryland, the District of Columbia, Ohio, Indiana, Illinois, Michigan, Wisconsin, Minnesota, North Dakota, California; and in the dominion of Canada the provinces of Alberta and Ontario) (1741)

✝ the British Province (1742)

✝ the Southern Province of the Moravian Church in North America (North Carolina, South Carolina, Virginia, Florida, and Georgia) (1753)

✝ the Jamaica Province (1754)

✝ the Labrador Province (1771)

✝ the Nicaragua Province (1849)

✝ the Guyana Province (1878)

✝ the Alaska Province (1885)

✝ the Southern Tanzania Province (1891)

✝ the Western Tanzania Province (1897)

✝ the Honduras Province (1930)

✝ the South Western Tanzania Province (1978)

✝ the Costa Rica Province (1980)

MORAVIAN PROVINCES WORLDWIDE

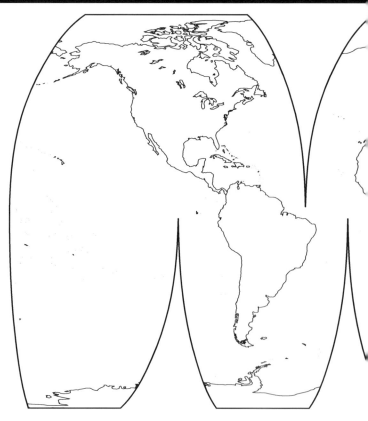

✝ the Rukwa Tanzania Province (1986)
✝ related work in northern India (1853)
✝ related work on Star Mountain, near Jerusalem (1981)
✝ related work in Siberia (1994)
✝ related work in Zaire (1994)
✝ related work in southern Mexico (2000)

Each *province* shares equally in the common faith, tradition, and witness of the church. The members of all the provinces are in partnership with one another. The goal of each province is to fulfill the calling of Christ in its life, worship, and organization. The largest groupings of Moravians live in Africa and Latin America.

Can you find the province of the worldwide Unity to which you belong? Who is the president of your Province? Can you identify who makes up the PEC of your province?

The Synod

The primary governing body for each *province* is the **Synod**. Representatives from the congregations along with pastors form **The Provincial Synod** and "vote according to their own conviction and are not bound by detailed instructions of their electors" (Book of Order, Article 403). At these meetings (in North America they are held every four years), *provinces* seek God's will to carry out the principles of the worldwide Moravian Church in teaching and practice. The *Provincial Synod* decides matters directly relating to living the faith in its particular area, and adapting it to the local conditions. They make decisions in regard to constitution, worship, and congregational life for its own province. They have oversight of affairs of the province administered in its behalf by the provincial board. The *Synod* elects bishops, delegates to the *Unity Synod,* and determines provincial undertakings and fields of work. The *Provincial Synod* serves as the final court of appeals for individual members or congregations.

Each *province* is encouraged to have the Scriptures and worship materials in a language with which congregations are familiar. Each *province* is responsible for training its own ministers and electing its own bishops. Some *provinces* are not yet able to supply their own needs and so enter into partnership with others. Each *province* works for the extension of the kingdom of God in its own area and wherever possible among people who do not belong to the race, nation, or language group of the majority of the members of the *province* concerned.

A **Provincial Board** is elected by the *Provincial Synod* to attend to provincial matters between Synodal gatherings. This elected body is known as **The Provincial Elders' Conference**, sometimes referred to as **The PEC**. They are responsible to carry out the church order and administer the *province* in keeping with the decisions of *Provincial Synod* and in view of the general tasks and objectives of the world Unity.

The Unity

The **Unity Synod** is that body which represents the *Unitas Fratrum* or Moravian Church as a whole. Members of the *Unity Synod* are members of the Church as a whole. They vote according to their own conviction and are not bound by detailed instructions of their electors. The *Unity Synod* determines general principles of the Unity of the Brethren in the world. The *Unity Synod* assigns the boundaries and respective spheres of work for each province of the Unity. They determine the principles governing our relationships as the Unity to other parts of the universal Christian Church. It is left to the *Unity Synod* to foster a common responsibility in regard to bringing the Gospel to bear on problems of contemporary life in the world. They serve as the final court of appeals in all matters concerning constitution, doctrine, congregational life, the ministry, and the spread of the Gospel.

The *Unity Synod* convenes every seven years. Between synods the **Unity Board**, comprised of one member from each provincial board (PEC), acts on behalf of the worldwide Unity. It is the responsibility of the Unity Board to uphold the further development of the Church in all parts of the world, to foster a spirit of unity in witness among the various provinces internationally, and to arrange for discussion of any divergent issues of faith among the Unity.

THE UNITY

UNITY SYNOD
Delegates Elected
by the Provinces

UNITY BOARD
One Member of Each
Provincial Board

THE PROVINCES

GROWTH ASSIGNMENT

Which province of the Unity of the Brethren are you drawn most toward? Spend some time praying for them, their work, and for those they hope to reach. Choose one part of the church's structure, and pray for God's Spirit to empower, enlighten, and guide them in all they do.

Chapter Eight

THE PERSONAL LIFE OF A DISCIPLE

MORAVIANS DESCRIBE what it's like to live as a follower of Jesus as a journey. We know where we're going, and who we're growing to resemble, but we haven't yet arrived. A poster's caption sums up how we view the Christian life: *"I'm not perfect...but God's not finished with me yet."* When Paul wrote to the Christians in Philippi he talked about the surpassing greatness of knowing Christ Jesus.

> *"I want to know Christ and the power of his resurrection and the fellowship of sharing in his sufferings, becoming like him in his death, and so, somehow, to attain the resurrection from the dead. Not that I have already obtained all this, or have already been made perfect, but I press on to take hold of that for which Christ Jesus took hold of me. Brothers, I do not consider myself yet to have taken hold of it. But one thing I do: Forgetting what is behind and straining toward what is ahead, I press on toward the goal to win the prize for which God has called me heavenward in Christ Jesus."*
>
> *Philippians 3:10-14 (NIV)*

We lay behind the sinful self, which Christ saved from eternal separation from God. We are no longer that same person who was dead in sin. So we commit ourselves to a *"growing up"* process. When John wrote his first letter he said,

> *"Beloved, we are God's children now; what we will be has not yet been revealed. What we do know is this: when he is revealed, we will be like him, for we will see him as he is. And all who have this hope in him purify themselves, just as he is pure."*
>
> 1 John 3:2-3 (NRSV)

GROWTH ASSIGNMENT

Can you remember some of the things you used to do apart from Christ? How has knowing Jesus made you different in your thoughts, words, and actions? Spend some time thanking God for His hand in shaping your character.

This maturing process is called **discipleship.** It is the last thing Jesus commanded us to do:

> *"Go therefore and make disciples of all nations, baptizing them in the name of the Father and of the Son and of the Holy Spirit, teaching them to observe all that I have commanded you; and lo, I am with you always, to the close of the age."*
>
> Matthew 28:19-20 (RSV)

Jesus saves us from sin and invites us to follow in His footsteps, learning to be more like Him. The process of learning as we go with Jesus makes us His *disciples,* or, *those who follow and learn.* We believe the commitment to live as a *disciple* is a daily decision and the most effective way truly to help others. *Discipleship* makes our Christian witness more powerful than words alone. Everything we do from the moment we accept Jesus as Savior becomes a reflection or witness of how thoroughly we're allowing Him to be Lord over all. When members are received into the church they are asked to profess their faith. The next question after affirming what they believe is, in a sense: *"Now what are you going to do because of what you believe?"*

"Do you in this faith turn away from sin, evil, and selfishness in your thoughts, words, and actions; and do you intend to participate actively in Christ's church, serving God all the days of your life?"
(Moravian Book of Worship, page 171)

Good intentions alone are not enough to build a healthy Christian community. In fact, Herrnhut had become marked by such bitter fighting that some members of the community actually moved out of town and prayed for God to destroy the others. Fortunately, they realized that Jesus was not being honored and the only witness they provided was to their pride and selfish ambition. They agreed to study and pray together to reach agreement on how they would treat one another regardless of how they felt. The motivation for their *covenant* agreement was not good feelings, but a commitment to be *disciples* of Jesus toward one another. Out of these sessions, Zinzendorf drafted a list of biblical principles necessary for Jesus to be reflected through their life together. As Zinzendorf compared their agreement to the disciplines of the *Ancient Unity* of the 15th century, all were amazed at the similarities. Originally named *The Brotherly Agreement*, we know it today as **The Moravian Covenant for Christian Living.**

There is always a danger in trying to be too specific in suggesting methods or exercises to develop one's faith. Even the best method can become an empty form if we are not prompted by the heartfelt desire to become more like Christ. But many Christians have found it helpful to follow spiritual principles to stimulate and ensure healthy spiritual growth. *The Moravian Covenant For Christian Living* is offered, not as a law of behavior, but as a guideline toward Christ-likeness in all we think, do, and say. New members who join congregations are asked to commit toward such an aim. Please refer to a copy of *The Moravian Covenant For Christian Living* as we proceed.

The Ground Of Our Witness

We want every aspect of our lives to point people to Christ. A healthy life of faith is centered on the person of Jesus, and based in the Scriptures as the source of information on how to live like Him in this world. Giving meaningful expression to the presence and power of Christ at work in and through us is the best way we know to help others experience God personally. Living as disciples of Jesus is our *witness* to the truth of God's power to change lives forever. People who know you best will be watching to see how genuine your walk with God is. You are already witnessing to what you have heard and seen of the Lord in your personal behavior.

GROWTH ASSIGNMENT

How do you think you are doing so far? What would those who know you best say is most important in your life? Reflect on your responsibility to witness to others.

The Witness Of The Christian Life

The first step in discipleship is developing and maintaining a healthy personal relationship with Jesus. We grow in Christ-likeness through certain exercises of faith such as prayer, devotions, study, and opportunities for spiritual development. It is said that couples who have been married long enough begin to resemble one another. Since Christians declare that Jesus will be our dearest friend, it is vital that we learn to spend regular time cultivating this friendship. The following are some disciplines to strengthen our growth in Christ.

Prayer - Many people imagine that prayer is talking to God. It is tempting to come to God with a list of things we want Him to do. Our attitude can be that God is some sort of heavenly Santa Claus and that we must get His attention to do things we are concerned about. But prayer is a conversation **with** God. If we search the Scriptures, it doesn't take long to discover that God has much more to say to us than we to Him. In fact, when Jesus taught His disciples to pray He began with a focus on the person and things of God.

> *This, then, is how you should pray: "Our Father in heaven, hallowed be your name, your kingdom come, your will be done on earth as it is in heaven. Give us today our daily bread. Forgive us our debts, as we also have forgiven our debtors. And lead us not into temptation, but deliver us from the evil one.*
>
> Matthew 6:9-13 (NIV)

Prayer always begins with God. God is the most important part of prayer. Setting aside a specific time that helps you to focus on the Lord without interruption will be helpful. If you've never prayed before, begin by simply setting aside a few minutes. Ask God to help grow your conversations with Him. A simple acronym to follow as a daily routine to pray is: **A C T S** - Adoration - Confession - Thanksgiving - Supplication.

Adoration is telling God how much you love Him. If words come easily and genuinely, tell God how much you love Him. Others find reading scripture, especially the Psalms, singing hymns, and even sitting in stillness helps express just how supremely important God is in our lives. Some find a daily devotional guide helpful to focus attention on God. *The Moravian Daily Texts* was developed to direct our hearts to God with a simple Old Testament and New Testament scripture. Use whatever tool connects you best to God.

Confession is agreeing with God that specific parts of our lives need to change. As we gain a clearer picture of who God is, we also discover where our lives do not measure up to the perfection of the Lord. God helps to heal our distance from Himself and others through the work of His Holy Spirit *convicting* us of the truth - we are sinners daily in need of grace. *Confession* allows us opportunity to clean house. We can ask God to take away our sins of thought, word, and deed. Confession allows us to remove any obstacles to growth in God by asking Christ to deal with our sin, which we are powerless to change.

If we claim to be without sin, we deceive ourselves and the truth is not in us. If we confess our sins, he is faithful and just and will forgive us our sins and purify us from all unrighteousness. If we claim we have not sinned, we make him out to be a liar and his word has no place in our lives. My dear children, I write this to you so that you will not sin. But if anybody does sin, we have one who speaks to the Father in our defense - Jesus Christ, the Righteous One.

1 John 1:8-2:1 (NIV)

Thanksgiving is counting the blessings received from God. As we talk specifically with the Lord about the places we recognize His hand in great and small ways, God is magnified, He becomes greater to us. By consistently living in a spirit of acknowledging God all around us, we have reason to rejoice. As God becomes greater, our problems and obstacles to growth become less.

Supplication is what we ask God to do. Your personal requests are not unimportant. But when compared to the things of God, it is possible that we may miss the Lord's good will if we only begin with ourselves. One reason we find our prayers unanswered is because we have asked with wrong motives (James 4:3-10). However, since we started in prayer *with* God, we are more likely to be thinking God's thoughts when it comes to asking the Lord to move in specific ways. It is possible that the Lord will prompt you to pray or intercede on behalf of someone else. Sometimes our issues are relieved simply by giving them to the Lord because we know He is God and bigger than our problems. Talk to your dearest friend, who already loves you and gave His life for you. One woman kept an empty chair next to her bed for the Lord when she spoke with Him. Some find it helpful to keep a list of those people and items the Lord brings to mind. Reflecting over the list provides ample opportunity to see how God works over time in very specific ways. Once you have made the Lord your *Chief Object*, you are encouraged to ask God to do whatever is in your heart. Jesus said:

"Ask and it will be given to you; search, and you will find; knock, and the door will be opened for you. For everyone who asks, receives, and everyone who searches finds, and for everyone who knocks, the door will be opened."

Matthew 7:7-8 (NRSV)

As you grow in your personal relationship with Jesus, God may also extend the amount of time you find yourself committing to prayer and devotion. Let God grow you until it becomes almost as essential as breathing. An increase in your desire to pray is a sign of deepening spiritual health. The Apostle Paul saw it so vital to Christian living, he called us to:

"Rejoice always; pray without ceasing; in everything give thanks; for this is the will of God in Christ Jesus for you."

1 Thessalonians 5:16-18 (NKJV)

Bible Reading

The source of information for growing into the likeness of our Savior is the Bible. It is like our spiritual protein supply. To neglect the Bible as a regular part of our life is to become malnourished in faith. Without the Scriptures, we have no solid standard of measure to be sure our growth matches the character of God. Many young Christians refrain from studying the Bible because they don't know enough about it. Somewhere inside they feel since they are Christians, they should automatically know it. The very means to overcoming their lack of information is kept out of reach. The best way to grow in the knowledge of God's Word is to become familiar with it. There are many ways to do so. Simply exposing ourselves to the Scriptures has an influence on us. Moravians believe this so sincerely that in *The Moravian Daily Texts* devotions and blessings, scripture verses are shared for consideration as gifts from the Lord.

> *All scripture is inspired by God and is useful for teaching, for reproof, for correction, and for training in righteousness, so that everyone who belongs to God may be proficient, equipped for every good work.*
> 2 Timothy 3:16-17 (NRSV)

In order to take in and grow in understanding God's Word there are several habits that may be helpful. If you've never read the Bible before, start in the Gospel accounts of **Luke** or **John** to learn first about Jesus. Then move to **Romans** or the letter of **1 John** to see the basics early Christians needed to know. After you grow to know the source personally, the rest of the story makes better sense. The following five methods (so you can count them on your fingers) describe how to get the most from your time with the Scriptures:

Hear - listening to sermons, readings, or interpretations from the Bible is probably how we were first introduced to God's Word. The difficulty with hearing is that we retain so little of the information we merely hear.
(Romans 10:17)

Read - simply reading the Bible for face value will familiarize you with what it says. Seeing it with our eyes paints indelible pictures of the things of God.
(Psalm 119:105)

Study - Here we seek to learn everything we can about the Bible. Knowledge of the larger biblical world and the deeper meanings of words can be a valuable source of better understanding God's work in human lives. A word of caution, however, concerning books about the Bible, while they serve a wonderful purpose in presenting additional information surrounding the texts of scripture, they are not the Scriptures. There is no substitute for the Word itself.

(Ezra 7:8-10)

Memorize - While we may remember only a fraction of what we hear or read, memorizing scripture gives us 100% retention. Before the Scriptures were written, vast sections of the Bible were passed along in memorized form. You can see this in the poetic nature of many passages. Memorizing a text lets you carry it with you wherever you go in anticipation of opportunities to share it.

(Deuteronomy 6:4-12)

Meditate - This is like chewing on a passage of the Bible to get out everything we can. Instead of focusing on what the Bible says, we hope to glimpse more deeply into what God means and how we might apply His revelation in our living.

(Psalm 119:97)

GROWTH ASSIGNMENT

What are some of your initial feelings about growing in your knowledge of God's Word? What might be the benefits to you of becoming more familiar with what God has to say? Schedule a time to talk with your pastor or someone you know who spends time in God's Word to help you begin.

The Witness Of A Living Church

The way we get along with one another tells the world all it needs to know about who is at work among us. While it is simple to keep secret the things of our hearts as individuals, the way we treat one another as a body is evidence of whether we live directed by God, or by our selfish desires.

By this shall all men know that ye are my disciples, if ye have love one to another.

John 13:35 (KJV)

Authority In The Church

The best leadership in the Church is that which serves. Jesus taught:

> *"You know that those who are regarded as rulers of the Gentiles lord it over them, and their high officials exercise authority over them. Not so with you. Instead, whoever wants to become great among you must be your servant, and whoever wants to be first must be slave of all."*
>
> *Mark 10:42-44 (NIV)*

The structures and people in positions of authority for the Moravian Church are our present best attempt to serve the Body of Christ as it follows its call. We understand that those in leadership over congregations and provinces are sinners in need of God's grace and mercy, like ourselves. We commit to pray for them that they may grow in Christ-likeness and God's fruit as they serve. When there are disagreements, we promise to submit ourselves to the decisions made by the larger church while we covenant to work matters out within the context of the body.

Stewardship

Everything we have and are is a gift from God. God blesses us abundantly to see how we might use the gifts He has entrusted to us in *time, talent, and treasure.* The way we use these gifts reflects our priorities in this world. When Jesus was asked about the greatest priority, He responded:

> *"Love the Lord your God with all your heart and with all your soul and with all your mind and with all your strength. The second is this: Love your neighbor as yourself. There is no commandment greater than these."*
>
> *Mark 12:30-31 (NIV)*

Jesus summarized the understanding of all the Scriptures when He simplified the kind of response God most desires from us: God gives us all that we are and all that we have to see if we will honor Him and be about His business. Let's look at the three types of gifts God entrusts into our hands for His glory: time, talent, and treasure.

Time - each of us has been given only 24 hours in each day. We no longer have yesterday, and haven't yet received tomorrow. We only have today, and God gives us the opportunity to use it to the best eternal consequences. Have you thought recently about how you prioritize your time?

GROWTH ASSIGNMENT

In light of all you have been learning about God's will, how would you arrange the following areas of your life: self, work/school, family, God, social relationships, church, other?

What would be a possible reason there could be a difference between God and church? Can you imagine how someone could actually spend too much time at church?

Prayerful monitoring of how we spend our time for God can actually help us know whether to say *"yes" or "no"* to additional opportunities to serve. Busy people are not necessarily pleasing or helpful to God.

Another way in which time becomes a gift from God is in the level of your *Christian maturity.* Over time and experience in faith your level of maturity and wisdom should increase. The kinds of activities you would consider to serve God may change. Can you understand why it might be a mistake to ask a new Christian to be an Elder or Trustee?

GROWTH ASSIGNMENT

What benefits could church leaders gain by seeking the advice of the older saints? If you were to look at your maturity of faith as a human life development, would you be: infant, toddler, child, adolescent, young adult, middle-aged adult, older adult? How well are you using your maturity in the things you do for God? The way we invest our time tells the world a great deal about what really matters in our life for Jesus. What are you saying is most important in the use of your time?

Talent - at birth every human being received certain abilities to survive in this world. They were God's gifts to every single person.

GROWTH ASSIGNMENT

Do you know what some of your natural abilities are? Have you ever taken time to thank God for giving them to you? Have you used those talents to serve God?

Another area of talent is in how people process information. It is as though everyone is *"wired"* differently. Some draw their energy by being in front of crowds; others do better when left alone to carefully work things through. Some base decisions on feelings, others, strictly on logic. Some people are very organized and methodical, while others seem to fly by the seat of their pants. These are all **temperaments** and describe not right or wrong, but the different ways people process information. God made us each different for a reason.

For example, a certain woman is straightforward and blunt. She would never put up with a purchase that wasn't absolutely to her liking. Store managers all know her. Her husband, on the other hand, has a much softer approach to confrontation. He asks about the family life of store workers and eventually gets around to deciding it would hurt their feelings too much if he were to return a purchased item. So, the husband goes home with something he doesn't want. The wonderful thing in the Body of Christ is that both types are needed. The woman helps her husband face the truth head on and get things done. The man, on the other hand, helps his wife to do it in a way that maintains a witness of love and affection for relationships to continue to grow.

The most difficult conflicts we face in life are when different personality types clash, without recognizing the true value each plays in the function of the church. God may want to change or modify problematic personality types. There may also be some traits to be developed you feel would help your witness.

Who are some people you know who seem to do better as a team than the sum of the individuals? Are there any "temperament" issues you would like God to grow, change, or modify in yourself?

In addition to talents, those who receive salvation in Jesus are promised *gifts from the Holy Spirit*. These gifts are provided to help redeemed sinners to do the work of the kingdom of God.

What spiritual gifts does the Bible talk about in Romans 12:3-8?
• 1 Corinthians 12:27-13:13?
• Ephesians 4:1-11?
• 1 Peter 4:10?
• Others?
Do any of these gifts sound like you?

As you consider joining a congregation there will be many invitations to consider offering yourself in service. One helpful guide in knowing what God wants you to do, or not do, is in your gifts. Since spiritual gifts are abilities that come as "grace gifts" from God, they express God's will for your life. Are there any areas of your life where you seem to bear unusual fruitfulness for God? When do you find the fruit of the Spirit bubbling to the surface as evidence of where God wants you?

> "But the harvest of the Spirit is love, joy, peace, patience, kindness, goodness, fidelity, gentleness, and self control."
> *Galations 5:22-23a (NEB)*

However, if you know without a shadow of a doubt that your gifts are not in teaching, then in joy you can say *"no"* when the Sunday School calls looking for teachers. If you are not sure, it is a good practice of faith to learn more about your gifts and to commit to experiment using them for a given time. At the end, have some trusted believers give you loving and honest feedback. Is the perceived gift an area you need to explore more, or can you look elsewhere?

If you are not using your gifts for God, your Christian life will lack the joy and sense of fulfillment God intends you to know. The whole Church will suffer because a part of the body God meant to be functioning is not yet on line. Perhaps you can see gifts at work in others and they don't realize it.

GROWTH ASSIGNMENT

Are there areas of church life where gifts are needed, but not apparent? Have you considered praying for God to send such gifts?

Now the big question for you personally: what should you do for God? You have examined yourself to have at least a preliminary understanding of how God has put you together for service. You are aware of your time availability, your maturity, and some measure of your talents and gifts. What opportunities are there in the congregation? If there is an inventory of ministries for your church, it would be helpful to pray through the opportunities with your profile in mind. Those items most suited to your abilities and which would give you the most joy are the best ones with which to begin. If there are no ministries in the congregation to utilize your gifts, it would be wise to talk with the pastor or other trusted leader for advice and direction toward ministry beyond the local church.

> **Treasure** - God never asks us to give what He hasn't already provided. Everything we have comes from God. The Bible teaches that the way to acknowledge we trust God for all we need is by giving to Him our first fruits. Giving allows the Church to carry on the business of our Savior in the world. In the Bible, the primary standard of giving was the tithe - the first tenth of everything. The tithe was God's way of taking care of the Temple and the people who led the worship for Israel.

Giving is to be as regular as we receive our sustenance. Giving is to God, not the budget or the Church. Giving is without strings attached, like God's love is to us. Giving is to be cheerfully and generously done, because in it we have the privilege to practice being like God in providing for others. The purpose of the *tithe* was specifically to meet the costs of Temple life and the welfare of the priests. According to **Malachi,** true giving doesn't begin until we have *tithed.* It becomes a sort of test of how good God can be if we trust Him enough to *tithe,* and beyond.

> *"Bring the whole tithe into the storehouse, that there may be food in my house, and test me now in this," says the Lord of hosts, "if I will not open for you the windows of heaven, and pour out for you a blessing until it overflows.'"*
> *Malachi 3:10 (NAS)*

There is a spiritual connection to what we do with money. When we give money to God, we are freed from its power over us and thus can better love the Lord with all our heart. When we worry about holding on to money, Jesus teaches that it gets a hold on us:

> *"No servant can serve two masters; for either he will hate the one and love the other, or he will be devoted to the one and despise the other. You cannot serve both God and mammon [material things]."*
> *Luke 16:13 (RSV)*

This may seem like an attempt to get your money. Actually, in light of our conversation it's an invitation to consider growing in your relationship and trust of God. When you can offer to God what you know in your heart only He made possible, God is magnified before you, and you receive the blessing of knowing how much He has cared for you. You cannot out-give the Lord. Tithing is not a law in the Moravian Church. It is a biblical principle for responding to the Lord's goodness. It is our faithful action to put our treasure where we want our hearts to be.

> *For where your treasure is, there will your heart be also.*
> *Matthew 6:21 (KJV)*

Each member is asked to determine prayerfully what is his/her ability to give. Giving large amounts of money does not mean a person's heart is right with God. Many rich people in Jesus' day gave their tithe religiously, but didn't trust God for it. However, the poor who gave what little they had amazed Jesus. They were willing to risk a much greater portion of their livelihood simply to love and honor the Lord.

We will not argue over whether you figure your giving before or after taxes, on gross or net. It is not our concern to determine what portion of your giving goes to congregational ministry as opposed to denominational, missions, benevolence, or other worthy causes outside the church. These are matters between you and your Savior. The most important concern is that you are giving to glorify God and grow in your loving trust of Him. What you do with your money sends a message to the world of what most matters in your life.

> *"Remember this; Whoever sows sparingly will also reap sparingly, and whoever sows generously will also reap generously. Each man should give what he has decided in his heart to give, not reluctantly or under compulsion, for God loves a cheerful giver. And God is able to make all grace abound to you, so that in all things at all times, having all that you need, you will abound in every good work. As it is written:*
>> *"He has scattered abroad his gift to the poor;*
>> *his righteousness endures forever."*
> *Now he who supplies seed to the sower and bread for food will also supply and increase your store of seed and will enlarge the harvest of your righteousness. You will be made rich in every way so that you can be generous on every occasion, and through us your generosity will result in thanksgiving to God."*
>
> *2 Corinthians 9:6-11 (NIV)*

When is the last time you prayed over your financial priorities? Are there any changes God might be asking you to make in the way you spend money? What other "treasures" has God placed in your life to steward? What would happen to you if you began tithing? What would your neighbors say is most important to you in the use of your material wealth?

Personal Relationships

Since the disciples of Jesus are to be known by the love they have for one another (John 13:35), we will cherish Christian love as of prime importance. We are eager to maintain the unity of the Church. This is especially challenging when we realize the diversity of backgrounds and opinions represented in any group of believers. We thank God for the rich variety of gifts and experiences of God represented among the Church. These are given to build us all up. However, when the differences divide, we covenant to work out our problems until unity is restored or the difficulty is determined to be irreconcilable. The world is watching how the Christian Church settles its differences. The validity of our witness hangs in the balance.

When there is a problem between two Christians, Jesus gives a simple rule of thumb method for reconciliation:

> *"If your brother sins against you, go and show him his fault, just between the two of you. If he listens to you, you have won your brother over. But if he will not listen, take one or two others along, so that 'every matter may be established by the testimony of two or three witnesses.' If he refuses to listen to them, tell it to the church; and if he refuses to listen even to the church, treat him as you would a pagan or a tax collector."*
>
> *Matthew 18:15-17 (NIV)*

Jesus says the person who has been offended is to go personally and directly to the other, with the goal of healing the division. There is no need to discuss with others, or to gossip. Each delay and additional person consulted enlarges the wound. Most disruptions to church harmony would be solved simply if each person accepted this responsibility. Only when unsuccessful in healing the relationship do we enlarge the sphere of people involved. The primary concerns throughout are our desire for repentance and forgiveness from sin, restored unity, and our consideration for the conclusion the world will draw about the Gospel as it observes. It is easy to become angry and storm away from conflict. It is extremely difficult to repair a damaged witness.

GROWTH ASSIGNMENT

What are some attitudes you are aware of from having observed churches deal with conflict? What is the most difficult step for you to imagine in reconciling a broken relationship? Are you involved in any Christian relationships that may need Jesus' advice and healing? Why not ask God to help reconcile His Body?

Worship

We have already spoken much about worship. It is included here again to reinforce the importance of our regular participation. While God is the center of worship and our role is to serve Him there, we also are a blessing to others through our participation. When we are present, the whole Church is built up from our gifts at work and we personally benefit from the renewing fellowship of the Holy Spirit. When we are absent, we, and the whole body suffer.

> *And let us consider one another in order to stir up love and good works, not forsaking the assembling of ourselves together, as is the manner of some, but exhorting one another, and so much the more as you see the Day approaching.*
>
> *Hebrews 10:24-25 (NKJV)*

Unity With Other Christians

Since the Moravian Church does not view itself as holding exclusive insight into the deep things of God, we actively seek to have fellowship with other Christian churches. We treat other believers with the same openness as we do members of the Unity. We view other Christian churches as our full brothers and sisters in the Lord Jesus Christ. We see them as sharing in the work of God's kingdom, rather than as competition. We ache over the broken condition of the Christian Church today, and pray with the Lord Jesus Christ:

> *I do not pray for these only, but also for those who believe in me through their word, that they may all be one; even as thou, Father, art in me, and I in thee, that they also may be in us, so that the world may believe that thou hast sent me.*
>
> *John 17:20-21 (RSV)*

The world's ability to believe is affected by our attitudes and actions toward one another in the Body of Jesus Christ.

GROWTH ASSIGNMENT

Who are some other Christian churches with which you are familiar? Why not take a few moments to pray for God to bless them in their ministry for Jesus?

The Witness Of The Christian Home

Marriage And Family

In the New Testament marriage is used to describe the relationship of Christ to the Church. We have an opportunity to witness to the love of Jesus by how we bring Christ to one another in marriage.

> *In the same way, husbands should love their wives as they do their own bodies. He who loves his wife loves*

himself. For no one ever hates his own body, but he nourishes and tenderly cares for it, just as Christ does for the church, because we are members of his body. "For this reason a man will leave his father and mother and be joined to his wife, and the two will become one flesh." This is a great mystery, and I am applying it to Christ and the church. Each of you, however, should love his wife as himself, and a wife should respect her husband.

Ephesians 5:28-33 (NRSV)

Marriage is God's idea. It is the one human relationship wherein the Lord intends for us to experience an approximation of His intimate love for us. In fact, in God's eyes, the closeness of marital love makes a husband and wife one. A new life comes into being as God joins a couple together and provides the foundation of stability for children and a beacon of encouragement for those who feel isolated and alone.

"Haven't you read," he replied, "At the beginning the Creator 'made them male and female,' and said, 'For this reason a man will leave his father and mother and be united to his wife, and the two will become one flesh'? So they are no longer two, but one. Therefore what God has joined together, let man not separate."

Matthew 19:4-6 (NIV)

The sad fact in America today is that Christian marriages statistically fare no better than non-Christian marriages. Such a reality suggests that our witness is suffering. The bottom line is that marriage is difficult. The pain of mistakes and relational failure are a crushing obstacle to experiencing the liberating love of God. It is hard to imagine Good News when locked in the despair of a broken marriage. Our culture tempts us to take our unfulfilled expectations for love and salve our wounds with others outside marriage. What the world needs desperately are models, not made in Hollywood, but on knees of contrition. Selfishness and pride are incompatible with the selfless and humble love of God, and therefore undo the union God intends whole.

> He said to them, "Because of your hardness of heart, Moses permitted you to divorce your wives; but from the beginning it has not been this way. And I say to you, whoever divorces his wife, except for immorality, and marries another woman commits adultery."
> Matthew 19:8-9 (NAS)

It is not against the law to formally end marriage in divorce. It is permissible in the Law of Moses. Even Jesus demonstrates how unfaithfulness is reasonable cause to end a marriage. But God means for marriage to demonstrate the best human love. Unfortunately, we too often bring to marriage and receive from it our human worst. Because God paints marriage to mirror His love for us, divorce displays the ultimate picture of sin: something broken apart that God meant to be together. If you are reading this now and have been divorced, or are in a troubled marriage, the message is not one of *condemnation*, but rather, an invitation for you to experience God's love anew, and therefore, to rediscover why God considers marriage such an important human relationship.

Since so many marriages in America end in divorce, the Church has a tremendous witness to those suffering from its devastating consequences. The Body of Christ is to be a haven for the divorced, just as it is a hospital for all sinners who are being saved by grace. It is the place to unload the pain, the weight of sin, the consequences of abuse, and the shame of failure in confession at Jesus' feet and know the arms of the Savior lifting you up in forgiveness. The Church is to be the people who do not lower the standard of God's teaching about marriage, but rather, raise up the greater grace of Jesus, which helps us begin again.

It may be necessary for us to reconsider the influence our culture and media have had on our expectations of Christian marriage. When we add to marriage the condition of the Christian family, it is clear that the Church has much work to do if our families are to demonstrate the power of God in our homes. If there is no godly difference at work among us, not only are we little help to others, but we also become part of the problem. Paul wrote to Timothy with caution about how important a healthy home life is as a prerequisite for leadership in the church.

If anyone does not know how to manage his own family, how can he take care of God's church?

1 Timothy 3:5 (NIV)

GROWTH ASSIGNMENT

Make a list of your expectations of marriage and family love and intimacy. Now identify which of these are biblical expectations and which are cultural. Are there any you might want to ask God's help in discarding or changing?

Part of our witness is to nurture and care for our marriages as we would a living person. They need nourishment, time, tender affection, good communication, and when they are sick, they need professional attention. Your pastor would be a good source of help if you feel your marriage witness could be better. Bible studies and support groups also specialize in providing a place to grow in an understanding of biblical marriage, to recover from divorce, the death of a loved one, or even abuse. Christian marriages can learn to demonstrate to their children, neighbors, and especially their spouses that it is possible to die to selfishness, and put on Christ toward our mates. When we offer the love, not of romance, but of Jesus, who gave His life for His friends, to one another in marriage, then, and only then, do we have the power to create a pattern for a relationship that will last and grow regardless of circumstance.

"In Scripture our Lord teaches us that from the beginning God made us male and female, and blessed the coming together of husband and wife so that the two should become one; that marriage is therefore a holy relationship; that Christians should be subject to one another out of reverence for Christ, love one another, be

faithful to one another, bear one another's weaknesses and limitations, forgive one another, cherish one another in joy and sorrow, pray for and encourage one another in all things, and live together as heirs of grace of life."
(Moravian Book of Worship, page 175)

GROWTH ASSIGNMENT

What are the influences that have significantly affected your family? How has responsibility for moral decision-making changed in your home over the years? What is the greatest need you might ask God to help with in your home and those closest to you? Where do the divorced find a place here?

One way to build a stronger family life is through daily sharing and devotions. The primary place children will learn about God is at home. By the time they are five years old most of the child's adult attitudes have already been formed through watching others in the home. The first witness we have is to our children. The key location of Christian Education is not Sunday School, but your home.

Train up a child in the way he should go, and when he is old he will not depart from it.
Proverbs 22:6 (NKJV)

For many in our culture, family life has been so disrupted over the year, that group life in the Church becomes the only healthy family they know. Everyone needs intimate, good friends. Small fellowship groups can be a wonderful place to learn about God as you grow in friendship with others. You can be known and cared for more intimately than in a corporate worship or large group setting. Small groups are not meant to be a substitute for home life, but a place of growth to learn to build more godly homes. These groups may be study based, work or mission motivated, primarily for prayer, meeting specific personal needs, or strictly for cultivating relationships. The group can be a place to experiment using your gifts and to find others willing to be honest about how well you're doing in the Lord. It can be a place to receive love and healing or to offer prayer, hospitality, or compassion.

GROWTH ASSIGNMENT

What opportunities are there for growing in friendship with the Lord and others? Prayerfully consider which might be most helpful to grow your witness for Jesus?

One aspect of Moravian home life that may seem unusual is the regular use of prayer at meal times. While Jesus cautions us to refrain from calling attention to ourselves in public, we do hold it a sacred honor to remember God's goodness whenever we pause to eat. Extemporaneous and creative prayers are encouraged. Several traditional forms of mealtime blessings have developed over the years. They are often called "Moravian Blessings."

Spoken: *Come, Lord Jesus, our Guest to be,*
             And bless these gifts bestowed by Thee.
             Bless Thy(our) dear(loved) ones everywhere,
             And keep them in Thy loving care.

Sung to a variety of tunes:
             Be present at our table, Lord,
             Be here and everywhere adored.
             From Thine all bounteous hand, our food

GROWTH ASSIGNMENT

Do you have a time each day to invite God into your family life? Who would you need to talk to for ideas to help?

The Witness Of A Christian Citizen

We believe the way we interact with civil and government authorities has a direct affect on the witness to our region and nation. Whether we agree or disagree with political leadership, we are compelled to pray for God's guidance over the affairs of state. Rather than detracting from the political process, we deem it a privileged Christian responsibility to be active in voting our conscience in all elections. One way

God has to affect government decision-making is through the voice of His people. We do not make political statements, like faith statements, but hold each member accountable to follow God's leading in expression of Christian views, even to the point of holding public office.

Everyone must submit himself to the governing authorities, for there is no authority except that which God has established. The authorities that exist have been established by God. Consequently, he who rebels against the authority is rebelling against what God has instituted, and those who do so will bring judgment on themselves. For rulers hold no terror for those who do right, but for those who do wrong.

Romans 13:1-3 (NIV)

We so strongly believe that God placed our civil authorities above us that we consider it a privilege to pay our fair taxes and other obligations. The only exception is when government actions run directly contrary to the authority of God. One area where Moravians have historically exercised the appeal to a higher authority is in regard to bearing arms. Many Moravians have found it so contrary to the teachings of Jesus to participate in war they entered into *"conscientious objection."*

Tell us then, what is your opinion? Is it right to pay taxes to Caesar or not?' But Jesus, knowing their evil intent said, "You hypocrites, why are you trying to trap me? Show me the coin used for paying the tax." They brought him a denarius, and he asked them, "Whose portrait is this? And whose inscription?" "Caesar's," they replied. Then he said to them, "Give to Caesar what is Caesar's, and to God what is God's."

Matthew 22:17-21 (NIV)

GROWTH ASSIGNMENT

How could we pray for our local, national, and world leaders? What issues facing us today need divine wisdom and intervention? Are you aware of any issues God may be bringing to your attention for your consideration and involvement?

Our Witness In The World

Since God loved the world so much that He sent His only Son to save it, Moravians believe the world is still due to receive our love. We want to strive to demonstrate the love of Jesus, not only within the Church, but especially to non-believers, regardless of their attitude toward us or their life styles. We endeavor not to hate, despise, slander, or otherwise injure anyone because we know each one is the object of the Lord's affection. In fact, we have a growing concern for the world's salvation to such a degree that we ask God to place us in particularly overlooked or marginalized places of witness. It has long been a unique sense of our call to proclaim God's love to those not reached by others. We pray that God will open doors for even the most unlikely to receive the message of the Gospel.

GROWTH ASSIGNMENT

Are you aware of any groups of people who are difficult for you to love? What is God's attitude toward them? How could you pray for them? Are there any open doors where the message of Jesus may be welcomed?

> *But you shall receive power when the Holy Spirit has come upon you; and you shall be witnesses to me in Jerusalem, and in all Judea and Samaria, and to the end of the earth.*
>
> *Acts 1:8 (NKJV)*

We are each called to witness what Jesus has done in us, and if need be, to suffer for it. We witness in what we do and what we avoid doing. We witness whether we intend to or not. The only question is – toward whom will people be pointed through our witness? There are people you know right now who do not know Jesus as Lord and Savior.

List the names of persons you know under each category below who either don't know or would benefit to be reminded of the love of Jesus for them.

- Family
- Friends
- Neighbors
- Work
- In the marketplace
- Enemies
- Others

Why not spend a few minutes in prayer for each of them, that God might open doors for His Gospel into their lives?

Remember, the world is watching. We want to be sure that anything we do does not lead someone else into sin. We are called to be careful not to indulge in any activity to excess. When we cause others to fall away, it is our sin for not loving them in the name of Christ. We are not called to *"fix"* or *"convert"* unbelievers. Actually, we are sent out to announce what He has done in us, and to look for open doors to share the Good News of what only God could do for others. God does the changing of hearts. *"Witness"* is not a program of the Church. It is not something a small group of *"evangelists"* does for us. Witnessing is a demonstration of how each part of the Church lives and breathes and moves, remembering in public what Jesus has done.

So how is your witness?

At the beginning of our study we considered God's invitation to follow Him. At the end of our study the question and invitation is still the same. When Peter stood with Jesus after the resurrection, he was filled with many overwhelming thoughts. Maybe you feel a bit overwhelmed too. You've studied a great deal of information. Peter had actually done his learning with Jesus. Yet he was unable to move forward because he had failed Jesus, not once, but three times as His follower. but Jesus' call is not based on Peter's, or your, ability to "get it right." It's based on what Jesus can do in and through human lives who love Him enough to trust God. Jesus restored Peter to ministry by asking him three times if he was sure he loved Jesus. Then Jesus said to him: *"Follow me!"* John 21:19.

What about you?

About The Author

KEVIN C. FRACK

THERE HAS NEVER BEEN A TIME I have not known about the love of Jesus. Raised in a Moravian family in Pennsylvania and New Jersey, I asked Him into my heart while still a child. It is Christ who helps me to recognize the foolishness of my sin and self-centered living. As I grow in gratitude for His love and mercy toward us all, I am filled with hope and a passionate desire to proclaim His goodness. I truly believe God has great things in store for those who love Him!

First of His many gifts is my wife of twenty six years, Beth. She is my partner in every way for ministry and is a gifted children's songwriter, musician, and worship leader. We have two grown children, Seth and Serah, who are the joy of my life.

Prior to pastoral ministry I served several years as an agricultural missionary and community developer in Nicaragua and Honduras, among the Miskito Indians of the east Coast of Central America. We then served the Bruderheim Congregation in rural Alberta, Canada, from 1983-86; worked in new church development in Columbus, Ohio, from 1986-95; and have been privileged to serve the Ardmore congregation in Winston-Salem since 1995.

The Lord has given me a great burden to prepare the church for the awesome work of sharing Jesus with a wide variety of people prior to His coming again. But getting the bride dressed for the groom is often heartbreaking and far beyond any abilities I might once have claimed. I cannot fix the church, but I certainly can throw myself before the Lord and cry out for more of Him. *O God, transform the church, and let it begin with me!*

Therefore, I come before you fully enamored with the power and potential of the Lord Jesus to use each of us in His eternal purpose to save His lost children. I pray that Christ's Body is waking up to its true reason for being and look forward to experiencing more of the Savior's work as we worship Him together today.